ROBERT MUGABE

ROBERT MUGABE

Lorraine Eide

CHELSEA HOUSE PUBLISHERS
NEW YORK
PHILADELPHIA

Chelsea House Publishers
EDITOR-IN-CHIEF: Nancy Toff
EXECUTIVE EDITOR: Remmel T. Nunn
MANAGING EDITOR: Karyn Gullen Browne
COPY CHIEF: Juliann Barbato
PICTURE EDITOR: Adrian G. Allen
ART DIRECTOR: Maria Epes
MANUFACTURING MANAGER: Gerald Levine

World Leaders—Past & Present
SENIOR EDITOR: John W. Selfridge

Staff for ROBERT MUGABE
ASSOCIATE EDITOR: Jeff Klein
COPY EDITOR: Terrance Dolan
DEPUTY COPY CHIEF: Ellen Scordato
EDITORIAL ASSISTANT: Heather Lewis
PICTURE RESEARCHER: Emily Miller
ASSISTANT ART DIRECTOR: Laurie Jewell
DESIGNER: David Murray
PRODUCTION COORDINATOR: Joseph Romano
COVER ILLUSTRATION: Peter McCaffrey

First Printing

1 3 5 7 9 8 6 4 2

Library of Congress Cataloging in Publication Data

Eide, Lorraine.
Robert Mugabe.

(World leaders past & present)
Bibliography: p.
Includes index.
Summary: Presents a biography of the first prime minister
of Zimbabwe.

1. Mugabe, Robert Gabriel, 1924–   —Juvenile
literature. 2. Prime ministers—Zimbabwe—Biography—
Juvenile literature. 3. Zimbabwe—Politics and government—
Juvenile literature. [1. Mugabe, Robert Gabriel,
1924–   . 2. Prime ministers. 3. Zimbabwe—Politics
and government] I. Title. II. Series.
DT962.82.M83E34   1988   968.91′04′0924 [B]
[92]   87-32557

ISBN 1-55546-845-4
    0-7910-0590-9 (pbk.)

Contents

JOHN ADAMS
JOHN QUINCY ADAMS
KONRAD ADENAUER
ALEXANDER THE GREAT
SALVADOR ALLENDE
MARC ANTONY
CORAZON AQUINO
YASIR ARAFAT
KING ARTHUR
HAFEZ al-ASSAD
KEMAL ATATÜRK
ATTILA
CLEMENT ATTLEE
AUGUSTUS CAESAR
MENACHEM BEGIN
DAVID BEN-GURION
OTTO VON BISMARCK
LÉON BLUM
SIMON BOLÍVAR
CESARE BORGIA
WILLY BRANDT
LEONID BREZHNEV
JULIUS CAESAR
JOHN CALVIN
JIMMY CARTER
FIDEL CASTRO
CATHERINE THE GREAT
CHARLEMAGNE
CHIANG KAI-SHEK
WINSTON CHURCHILL
GEORGES CLEMENCEAU
CLEOPATRA
CONSTANTINE THE GREAT
HERNÁN CORTÉS
OLIVER CROMWELL
GEORGES-JACQUES
   DANTON
JEFFERSON DAVIS
MOSHE DAYAN
CHARLES DE GAULLE
EAMON DE VALERA
EUGENE DEBS
DENG XIAOPING
BENJAMIN DISRAELI
ALEXANDER DUBČEK
FRANÇOIS & JEAN-CLAUDE
   DUVALIER
DWIGHT EISENHOWER
ELEANOR OF AQUITAINE
ELIZABETH I
FAISAL
FERDINAND & ISABELLA
FRANCISCO FRANCO
BENJAMIN FRANKLIN

FREDERICK THE GREAT
INDIRA GANDHI
MOHANDAS GANDHI
GIUSEPPE GARIBALDI
AMIN & BASHIR GEMAYEL
GENGHIS KHAN
WILLIAM GLADSTONE
MIKHAIL GORBACHEV
ULYSSES S. GRANT
ERNESTO "CHE" GUEVARA
TENZIN GYATSO
ALEXANDER HAMILTON
DAG HAMMARSKJÖLD
HENRY VIII
HENRY OF NAVARRE
PAUL VON HINDENBURG
HIROHITO
ADOLF HITLER
HO CHI MINH
KING HUSSEIN
IVAN THE TERRIBLE
ANDREW JACKSON
JAMES I
WOJCIECH JARUZELSKI
THOMAS JEFFERSON
JOAN OF ARC
POPE JOHN XXIII
POPE JOHN PAUL II
LYNDON JOHNSON
BENITO JUÁREZ
JOHN KENNEDY
ROBERT KENNEDY
JOMO KENYATTA
AYATOLLAH KHOMEINI
NIKITA KHRUSHCHEV
KIM IL SUNG
MARTIN LUTHER KING, JR.
HENRY KISSINGER
KUBLAI KHAN
LAFAYETTE
ROBERT E. LEE
VLADIMIR LENIN
ABRAHAM LINCOLN
DAVID LLOYD GEORGE
LOUIS XIV
MARTIN LUTHER
JUDAS MACCABEUS
JAMES MADISON
NELSON & WINNIE
   MANDELA
MAO ZEDONG
FERDINAND MARCOS
GEORGE MARSHALL

MARY, QUEEN OF SCOTS
TOMÁS MASARYK
GOLDA MEIR
KLEMENS VON METTERNICH
JAMES MONROE
HOSNI MUBARAK
ROBERT MUGABE
BENITO MUSSOLINI
NAPOLÉON BONAPARTE
GAMAL ABDEL NASSER
JAWAHARLAL NEHRU
NERO
NICHOLAS II
RICHARD NIXON
KWAME NKRUMAH
DANIEL ORTEGA
MOHAMMED REZA PAHLAVI
THOMAS PAINE
CHARLES STEWART
   PARNELL
PERICLES
JUAN PERÓN
PETER THE GREAT
POL POT
MUAMMAR EL-QADDAFI
RONALD REAGAN
CARDINAL RICHELIEU
MAXIMILIEN ROBESPIERRE
ELEANOR ROOSEVELT
FRANKLIN ROOSEVELT
THEODORE ROOSEVELT
ANWAR SADAT
HAILE SELASSIE
PRINCE SIHANOUK
JAN SMUTS
JOSEPH STALIN
SUKARNO
SUN YAT-SEN
TAMERLANE
MOTHER TERESA
MARGARET THATCHER
JOSIP BROZ TITO
TOUSSAINT L'OUVERTURE
LEON TROTSKY
PIERRE TRUDEAU
HARRY TRUMAN
QUEEN VICTORIA
LECH WALESA
GEORGE WASHINGTON
CHAIM WEIZMANN
WOODROW WILSON
XERXES
EMILIANO ZAPATA
ZHOU ENLAI

CHELSEA HOUSE PUBLISHERS

ON LEADERSHIP

Arthur M. Schlesinger, jr.

LEADERSHIP, it may be said, is really what makes the world go round. Love no doubt smooths the passage; but love is a private transaction between consenting adults. Leadership is a public trans- action with history. The idea of leadership affirms the capacity of individuals to move, inspire, and mobilize masses of people so that they act together in pursuit of an end. Sometimes leadership serves good purposes, sometimes bad; but whether the end is benign or evil, great leaders are those men and women who leave their personal stamp on history.

Now, the very concept of leadership implies the proposition that individuals can make a difference. This proposition has never been universally accepted. From classical times to the present day, eminent thinkers have regarded individuals as no more than the agents and pawns of larger forces, whether the gods and goddesses of the ancient world or, in the modern era, race, class, nation, the dialectic, the will of the people, the spirit of the times, history itself. Against such forces, the individual dwindles into insignificance.

So contends the thesis of historical determinism. Tolstoy's great novel *War and Peace* offers a famous statement of the case. Why, Tolstoy asked, did millions of men in the Napoleonic Wars, denying their human feelings and their common sense, move back and forth across Europe slaughtering their fellows? "The war," Tol- stoy answered, "was bound to happen simply because it was bound to happen." All prior history predetermined it. As for leaders, they, Tolstoy said, "are but the labels that serve to give a name to an end and, like labels, they have the least possible connection with the event." The greater the leader, "the more conspicuous the inev- itability and the predestination of every act he commits." The leader, said Tolstoy, is "the slave of history."

Determinism takes many forms. Marxism is the determinism of class. Nazism the determinism of race. But the idea of men and women as the slaves of history runs athwart the deepest human instincts. Rigid determinism abolishes the idea of human freedom—

the assumption of free choice that underlies every move we make, every word we speak, every thought we think. It abolishes the idea of human responsibility, since it is manifestly unfair to reward or punish people for actions that are by definition beyond their control. No one can live consistently by any deterministic creed. The Marxist states prove this themselves by their extreme susceptibility to the cult of leadership.

More than that, history refutes the idea that individuals make no difference. In December 1931 a British politician crossing Park Avenue in New York City between 76th and 77th Streets around 10:30 P.M. looked in the wrong direction and was knocked down by an automobile—a moment, he later recalled, of a man aghast, a world aglare: "I do not understand why I was not broken like an eggshell or squashed like a gooseberry." Fourteen months later an American politician, sitting in an open car in Miami, Florida, was fired on by an assassin; the man beside him was hit. Those who believe that individuals make no difference to history might well ponder whether the next two decades would have been the same had Mario Constasino's car killed Winston Churchill in 1931 and Giuseppe Zangara's bullet killed Franklin Roosevelt in 1933. Suppose, in addition, that Adolf Hitler had been killed in the street fighting during the Munich *Putsch* of 1923 and that Lenin had died of typhus during World War I. What would the 20th century be like now?

For better or for worse, individuals do make a difference. "The notion that a people can run itself and its affairs anonymously," wrote the philosopher William James, "is now well known to be the silliest of absurdities. Mankind does nothing save through initiatives on the part of inventors, great or small, and imitation by the rest of us—these are the sole factors in human progress. Individuals of genius show the way, and set the patterns, which common people then adopt and follow."

Leadership, James suggests, means leadership in thought as well as in action. In the long run, leaders in thought may well make the greater difference to the world. But, as Woodrow Wilson once said, "Those only are leaders of men, in the general eye, who lead in action. . . . It is at their hands that new thought gets its translation into the crude language of deeds." Leaders in thought often invent in solitude and obscurity, leaving to later generations the tasks of imitation. Leaders in action—the leaders portrayed in this series—have to be effective in their own time.

And they cannot be effective by themselves. They must act in response to the rhythms of their age. Their genius must be adapted, in a phrase of William James's, "to the receptivities of the moment." Leaders are useless without followers. "There goes the mob," said the French politician hearing a clamor in the streets. "I am their leader. I must follow them." Great leaders turn the inchoate emotions of the mob to purposes of their own. They seize on the opportunities of their time, the hopes, fears, frustrations, crises, potentialities. They succeed when events have prepared the way for them, when the community is awaiting to be aroused, when they can provide the clarifying and organizing ideas. Leadership ignites the circuit between the individual and the mass and thereby alters history.

It may alter history for better or for worse. Leaders have been responsible for the most extravagant follies and most monstrous crimes that have beset suffering humanity. They have also been vital in such gains as humanity has made in individual freedom, religious and racial tolerance, social justice, and respect for human rights.

There is no sure way to tell in advance who is going to lead for good and who for evil. But a glance at the gallery of men and women in *World Leaders—Past and Present* suggests some useful tests.

One test is this: Do leaders lead by force or by persuasion? By command or by consent? Through most of history leadership was exercised by the divine right of authority. The duty of followers was to defer and to obey. "Theirs not to reason why / Theirs but to do and die." On occasion, as with the so-called enlightened despots of the 18th century in Europe, absolutist leadership was animated by humane purposes. More often, absolutism nourished the passion for domination, land, gold, and conquest and resulted in tyranny.

The great revolution of modern times has been the revolution of equality. The idea that all people should be equal in their legal condition has undermined the old structure of authority, hierarchy, and deference. The revolution of equality has had two contrary effects on the nature of leadership. For equality, as Alexis de Tocqueville pointed out in his great study *Democracy in America,* might mean equality in servitude as well as equality in freedom.

"I know of only two methods of establishing equality in the political world," Tocqueville wrote. "Rights must be given to every citizen, or none at all to anyone . . . save one, who is the master of all." There was no middle ground "between the sovereignty of all and the absolute power of one man." In his astonishing prediction of 20th-century totalitarian dictatorship, Tocqueville explained how the revolution of equality could lead to the *"Führerprinzip"* and more terrible absolutism than the world had ever known.

But when rights are given to every citizen and the sovereignty of all is established, the problem of leadership takes a new form, becomes more exacting than ever before. It is easy to issue commands and enforce them by the rope and the stake, the concentration camp and the *gulag.* It is much harder to use argument and achievement to overcome opposition and win consent. The Founding Fathers of the United States understood the difficulty. They believed that history had given them the opportunity to decide, as Alexander Hamilton wrote in the first Federalist Paper, whether men are indeed capable of basing government on "reflection and choice, or whether they are forever destined to depend . . . on accident and force."

Government by reflection and choice called for a new style of leadership and a new quality of followership. It required leaders to be responsive to popular concerns, and it required followers to be active and informed participants in the process. Democracy does not eliminate emotion from politics; sometimes it fosters demagoguery; but it is confident that, as the greatest of democratic leaders put it, you cannot fool all of the people all of the time. It measures leadership by results and retires those who overreach or falter or fail.

It is true that in the long run despots are measured by results too. But they can postpone the day of judgment, sometimes indefinitely, and in the meantime they can do infinite harm. It is also true that democracy is no guarantee of virtue and intelligence in government, for the voice of the people is not necessarily the voice of God. But democracy, by assuring the right of opposition, offers built-in resistance to the evils inherent in absolutism. As the theologian Reinhold Niebuhr summed it up, "Man's capacity for justice makes democracy possible, but man's inclination to injustice makes democracy necessary."

A second test for leadership is the end for which power is sought. When leaders have as their goal the supremacy of a master race or the promotion of totalitarian revolution or the acquisition and exploitation of colonies or the protection of greed and privilege or the preservation of personal power, it is likely that their leadership will do little to advance the cause of humanity. When their goal is the abolition of slavery, the liberation of women, the enlargement of opportunity for the poor and powerless, the extension of equal rights to racial minorities, the defense of the freedoms of expression and opposition, it is likely that their leadership will increase the sum of human liberty and welfare.

Leaders have done great harm to the world. They have also conferred great benefits. You will find both sorts in this series. Even "good" leaders must be regarded with a certain wariness. Leaders are not demigods; they put on their trousers one leg after another just like ordinary mortals. No leader is infallible, and every leader needs to be reminded of this at regular intervals. Irreverence irritates leaders but is their salvation. Unquestioning submission corrupts leaders and demeans followers. Making a cult of a leader is always a mistake. Fortunately hero worship generates its own antidote. "Every hero," said Emerson, "becomes a bore at last."

The signal benefit the great leaders confer is to embolden the rest of us to live according to our own best selves, to be active, insistent, and resolute in affirming our own sense of things. For great leaders attest to the reality of human freedom against the supposed inevitabilities of history. And they attest to the wisdom and power that may lie within the most unlikely of us, which is why Abraham Lincoln remains the supreme example of great leadership. A great leader, said Emerson, exhibits new possibilities to all humanity. "We feed on genius. . . . Great men exist that there may be greater men."

Great leaders, in short, justify themselves by emancipating and empowering their followers. So humanity struggles to master its destiny, remembering with Alexis de Tocqueville: "It is true that around every man a fatal circle is traced beyond which he cannot pass; but within the wide verge of that circle he is powerful and free; as it is with man, so with communities."

1

Detention

In 1964 Rhodesia was a self-governing British colony in southern Africa. Its white minority government, descendants of the British settlers who first took the land from the native Africans just 74 years before, was openly racist and had taken away most of the Africans' rights, even though they made up 95 percent of Rhodesia's total population. In the last few years blacks stepped up their protests against the government and its policies, but to no avail.

The prisoners of the Sikombela detention center rested for a few minutes, admiring the house they had built. True, it was nothing more than a cramped hut made of mud and thatched straw, and it would be cold on winter nights, but it was shelter nonetheless. The rule at Sikombela was that each prisoner had to build his own hut, so when the new prisoner who was arriving today, Robert Mugabe, saw that his hut was already built, he would know how much the other prisoners respected him.

There was not much else they could do for Mugabe. They were sure he would find life at Sikombela as miserable as they did. The camp, surrounded by barbed wire, was isolated in the midst of lonely bushland. Each detainee was given three blankets, khaki shorts, a short-sleeved shirt, an undershirt,

In his honour the Zanu detainees built him a home of his own—a thatched 'daja' hut with a door made painstakingly from reeds.
—DAVID SMITH
Mugabe biographer

A white Rhodesian policeman arrests a black protester in 1964. Blacks made up 95 percent of the population of Britain's southern African colony, but the white racist government that had held power for more than 70 years deprived blacks of most political, social, and economic rights.

White Rhodesian schoolchildren in the 1950s. The Rhodesian government allotted 10 times more funding for white education than for black education in its segregated school system, whereas 99 percent of Rhodesia's whites could read and write, the literacy rate for blacks was less than 30 percent.

and sometimes a jersey in the winter. They were not allowed to have shoes, and with only three blankets and no heat in the huts, the winter nights were so cold they could not sleep. They had no beds anyway; some slept on thin rope mats, some on the ground.

All the prisoners at Sikombela were political prisoners, detained because of their beliefs. The government divided them into three groups: Class I prisoners, who were white; Class II prisoners, who were Asian or of mixed race; and Class III prisoners, who were black. Class I prisoners received the best treatment, while Class III prisoners — the men who built the hut for Robert Mugabe — received the worst. Class III prisoners got the same meals almost every day — porridge for breakfast, porridge and beans for lunch, and a bit of meat and half-rotten vegetable, often crawling with maggots, for dinner.

Several of the Class III detainees had tuberculosis and all of them felt weak, tired, and listless. They had not seen any of their relatives since they had arrived at Sikombela. The prisoners sent letters, but they knew the guards threw many away instead of mailing them. They knew their families wrote faithfully, but the guards read the letters and usually destroyed those that contained anything more than word of family matters. Sometimes they got copies of newspapers and magazines, several weeks or months late, but again, any references to current news or politics were cut out. The prisoners had no idea what was going on in the world outside the camp.

All the detainees belonged to the same political party, the Zimbabwe African National Union; that was the offense for which they were being held at Sikombela. They joined the party, known as ZANU, because they believed that their country should be ruled by a black leader chosen in a democratic election. But under the laws of the white minority government, blacks were prohibited from joining political parties. Only a handful of blacks, those who had managed somehow to acquire wealth or an education, were allowed to vote in the elections. And only white people could run for office.

The exterior of a typical school for blacks under white Rhodesian rule. By the early 1960s the institutionalized racism of Rhodesian society had prompted black leaders to organize political parties and press their demands for equality. Robert Mugabe was one of many jailed for leading the effort.

A veteran of the 1896—97 African uprising against Rhodesia's first white settlers hands a ceremonial axe to black nationalist leader Joshua Nkomo (in hat at left) in 1962. Mugabe, then a rising young member of the nationalist movement, kneels immediately to the right of Nkomo. Both were jailed by the white government in 1963.

The blacks' situation in Rhodesia had been bad ever since the whites had arrived in the country. But bad as it was, it had deteriorated even more after 1962, when the whites in the colony had elected the ultraconservative Rhodesian Front to run the country. Under the leadership of Winston Field, the new government began to take away the few rights previous colonial governments had granted blacks. It became illegal for blacks to use the same facilities as whites, who had separate and much better neighborhoods, schools, hospitals, restaurants, transportation, and even public toilets. Most skilled jobs were reserved for whites. Wages for whites were kept artificially high, while wages for blacks were kept artificially low. Whites doing the same jobs as blacks could be paid several times as much. Most of the Rhodesian government's budget for education, health, and housing went to the whites.

Even worse was the British government's inability to pressure the Rhodesian Front. Every time the British protested about what the Front was doing, the party threatened to declare Rhodesia independent from Britain. The British seemed afraid to antagonize the Front into proclaiming Rhodesia's independence, and so were unwilling to protect the rights of the colony's black population.

For instance, under British colonial law, blacks were allowed to form political parties. But the Rhodesian Front overruled the law and banned black political parties almost as soon as they formed. The Front outlawed ZANU in 1964, only a year after it had been formed. Many of ZANU's leaders had been thrown into detention centers, including Sikombela. Under the Rhodesian Front government, one did not have to commit a crime or even threaten to commit a crime to be sent to a detention camp indefinitely; anyone the Front wanted in detention would simply be detained without charges and without the right to a trial.

A white farming couple in front of their home near Salisbury, the Rhodesian capital. Half of Rhodesia's total area — and most of its best land — was set aside for the whites' exclusive use. The prosperity enjoyed by white Rhodesians attracted thousands of British immigrants from 1945 to 1965.

In September 1964 the white regime took steps to control demonstrations by black nationalists. One of the measures was the temporary branding of blacks' palms; if anyone bearing the brand was found outside an area designated for blacks, he or she could be arrested.

The Sikombela prisoners had been detained for less than a year and already it seemed like a lifetime. The days seemed interminably long, with nothing to do and no end in sight. Mugabe, they knew, had been safely out of Rhodesia but had come back home deliberately to be arrested, and had already spent several months in jail. He had said he wanted his people to know he was willing to suffer the terrible conditions in Rhodesia with them. The prisoners admired him for that.

Mugabe finally arrived. He was not what they had expected. Instead of the commanding presence and the physical stature many associated with a nationalist leader who risked his life to stand at the forefront of the liberation movement, they saw a short, soft-spoken, bespectacled man. But almost instantly they could feel the quiet strength he exuded.

On his first day at the detention camp Mugabe told the prisoners that the struggle to transform white racist Rhodesia into independent black Zimbabwe would be arduous. They would be in Sikombela for years, perhaps decades. The people of Zimbabwe would not be able to rescue them, because there were no armies strong enough to challenge the government — yet. They had to keep faith that they would eventually succeed and use their years in prison to prepare for independence. "These months, these years, however long it takes, must not be wasted," he said.

Education was the first step. Unlike Mugabe, who already had more than one university degree, most of the prisoners either were illiterate or had not finished secondary school because the colonial government gave blacks very little access to education. Prisoners with some education would teach those without any in the mornings, and would themselves study in the afternoons. The prisoners chose their own teachers from among their ranks, and Mugabe was chosen to supervise all of the classes. He spent the entire day teaching, correcting work, and encouraging the prisoners; at night, he would work toward obtaining his correspondence-school law degree from the University of London. Usually he studied through the night and at sunrise would join the other prisoners in preparing breakfast and beginning morning classes. He seemed not to need the sleep, even though he was as weak as the other prisoners from lack of decent food.

For Mugabe, education meant more than learning to read and write. He also wanted the prisoners to discuss politics and learn to make political decisions together in preparation for the day they would govern the country. Although Mugabe was clearly a leader at Sikombela, he refused to impose decisions on the other prisoners. Nor did he encourage them to make decisions by voting and expecting the minority to conform to the majority's will. Instead, he urged the prisoners to discuss their differences and decide how they could be resolved so that a consensus could be reached. At first, it seemed like an unnecessarily long and frustrating process. But eventually the prisoners found that they were much more committed to these consensus decisions than to decisions reached by a vote.

In May 1965, about a year after Mugabe arrived, the prisoners noticed that security at Sikombela had been increased. Mugabe asked one of the guards why and learned that what he feared most had happened: In late 1964 the Rhodesian Front had found even Winston Field too liberal, so they

Rhodesian prime minister Ian Smith signing the Unilateral Declaration of Independence (UDI) in November 1965, after the country's whites had voted 10 to 1 in favor of the move. UDI made Rhodesia independent of Britain — and thus able to bypass Britain's pledge to replace the white regime with black majority rule.

The front page of a Rhodesian newspaper in 1965, with white space showing where articles had been removed by government censors. The UDI regime passed even stiffer measures against dissent than previous Rhodesian governments, prolonging the detention of black leaders and imposing increased press censorship.

forced him to resign and appointed Ian Smith to lead the party and the country. Now Smith had proclaimed Rhodesia's Unilateral Declaration of Independence (UDI) from Britain.

All remaining constraints on the racist government were gone. Under British rule, the Rhodesian Front could only ban those political parties they claimed were subversive. The members of banned parties could simply regroup under another party name and continue to protest to the British colonial government against the practice of white minority rule. Mugabe, for example, had joined several political parties in the early 1960s, each of which had been banned soon after it had been formed. During the brief time each party had been legal, he had been able to talk to large audiences and organize protests against specific government policies.

But now, under Smith's new UDI government, if anyone criticized the government or organized peaceful protests against government policy, the criticisms could be labeled treasonous and punishable by death. Smith would further reduce spending on education, health care, and housing for blacks while preventing the already low wages earned by blacks from rising.

If all peaceful means of protest were cut off, Mugabe and the other leaders of ZANU reasoned, violent methods remained their only option for introducing majority rule to the country. With most of the country's black leaders in detention, they decided that if it was necessary to fight a war from jail, they would do so. The prisoners had long ago made friends with some of the blacks who guarded the prison. Now they asked these guards to smuggle letters out to ZANU activists who were still free. They consulted by letter with an activist named Herbert Chitepo and encouraged him to organize a guerrilla army. Mugabe and the other prisoners decided to create a council of war, the *Dare re Chimurenga*, to carry on the activities of the party while its leaders were in jail.

Soon after the Unilateral Declaration of Independence, the guerrillas carried out their first serious military action, the killing of a white official who lived just 50 miles outside Salisbury, the Rhodesian capital. ZANU had made its point, and the white regime was shaken. Smith announced that Mugabe was to be transferred to the maximum security prison in Salisbury.

The Sikombela prisoners watched Mugabe leave the detention center. But strangely, they felt confident — or at least a lot more confident than they had been when he had first arrived. In two years he had transformed their desolate camp into a university and the headquarters of a war for independence. Clearly, they believed, a maximum security prison could not hinder Mugabe for long.

> *The routine, the orderliness and self-discipline Mugabe preached at Sikombela has remained his own hallmark.*
> —DAVID SMITH
> Mugabe biographer

2

Pioneers

About 1,000 years ago, in the middle of southern Africa, a great empire was born. Nothing remains of this empire but the ruins of some 400 stone buildings scattered throughout present-day Zimbabwe. The largest and most impressive of these ruins are the remnants of a large military, commercial, and religious center — an entire city, the oldest parts of which date from the 8th century and the newest from the 15th century.

Africans living near the site have always referred to it as *Zimbabwe*, a word in the Shona language literally meaning "burial ground of the chiefs," but which can be translated as "capital city." The people of the ancient empire constructed the massive buildings at Zimbabwe — located in the south-central portion of the modern country that bears the same name — from the gray stone quarried in the region, and by the time the last and greatest of them were built they had perfected the technique of cutting the stones to fit together perfectly without mortar or concrete. Gracefully curved stone staircases, arched doorways, and complex-patterned passageways and walls adorned the buildings.

The pioneers . . . paraded on the veld, and in the name of Queen Victoria formally took possession of Mashonaland, and all other unpossessed land in South-Central Africa that it should be found desireable to add to the Empire.
—W. D. GALE
historian

An 1895 cartoon depicting Cecil Rhodes as the builder of the British Empire in Africa. Rhodes became rich through diamond and gold mining in South Africa. He later conceived and led the effort to conquer and colonize Zimbabwe, which the white settlers named Rhodesia in his honor.

Part of the ruins of ancient Zimbabwe, the capital of an empire that flourished in southern Africa from the 10th to the 15th century. Sophisticated in commerce, art, and architecture, the city's name was chosen by 20th-century Rhodesian blacks for the black-ruled nation they envisioned.

The people of Zimbabwe carved imposing stone statues, painted delicate pictures, and produced beautiful, intricate jewelry of gold and copper. Their empire traded widely with the Arab city-states on the southeast coast of Africa and bought luxury goods from as far away as Persia, India, and China. Yet by the 16th century the empire had vanished, and to this day nobody knows why.

Around 1450 a new African empire had become dominant, the Mwanamutapa kingdom, situated on the Zambezi River along what is today Zimbabwe's northern border. The Mwanamutapa still ruled the region when the Portuguese arrived in 1569 to explore for trade and gold and became the first Europeans to make contact with the inhabitants of the Zimbabwean region. By 1693 malaria had forced the Portuguese to leave the region, but not before their encroachment had severely weakened the Mwanamutapa kingdom.

More than a century later the next major upheaval occurred. In the 1820s the armies of Shaka, a Zulu warrior from what is today South Africa, swept through much of the continent's southern area. Shaka offered the peoples he conquered equal status if they allied themselves with his Zulu empire, and one of his allies, the Ndebele people, established a powerful kingdom of their own. They conquered neighboring tribes and absorbed them into their ranks, but in 1837 white Afrikaner settlers — the descendants of Dutchmen who had come to southern Africa in the 17th century — arrived and drove out the Ndebele, who then headed for the rich lands to the north.

The Ndebele moved across the Limpopo River into southwestern Zimbabwe and defeated the people who lived there, the Shona, who were forced to pay their conquerors heavy taxes in the form of crops and cattle. By 1870 the Ndebele and their leader, Lobengula, had subjugated all of Zimbabwe and the Shona, who made up the majority of the country's population. The process of absorbing the Shona into the Ndebele community was well under way when another wave of European conquest interrupted it.

In 1888 Cecil Rhodes, a 35-year-old Englishman who as a young man had become one of the world's wealthiest people by investing in diamond mining in South Africa, set out to conquer Zimbabwe for the British Empire. A self-made man who strongly believed that the English-speaking nations were destined to rule the world, he had already engineered the extension of British rule from South Africa into Bechuanaland (present-day Botswana). Now, attracted by Zimbabwe's gold and other precious metals, and acting to prevent the Portuguese, Germans, and Afrikaners from establishing control in the region, Rhodes obtained a treaty from Lobengula entitling him to exclusive mineral rights for the entire country. In exchange Lobengula received rifles and ammunition for his armies. As part of the agreement, Rhodes's representatives promised the Ndebele chief that no more than 10 whites would enter the territory.

In 1889 Rhodes formed the British South Africa Company to administer his mining enterprise in Zimbabwe, build a rail link to South Africa, and colonize the country. One year later the colonization began, despite the objections of Lobengula — and far more than 10 whites were involved. A wagon train of 200 heavily armed British South African settlers, protected by 300 police, moved through the Ndebele lands of the southeast and into the Shona lands of

Ndebele warriors in 1835, in what is today the northeastern portion of South Africa. Two years after this illustration was made, white settlers arrived and forced the Ndebele to move north into Zimbabwe. There the Ndebele conquered the Shona, who had lived in Zimbabwe for centuries.

A 20th-century depiction of Lobengula, chief of the Ndebele, who in 1888 allowed Rhodes's representatives to set up mining operations in the country. Two years later, Rhodes, who had promised not to send more than 10 whites into Lobengula's lands, began the large-scale settlement of the territory.

the northwest, where they established their first settlement, Salisbury. Rhodes had chosen the 200 from a pool of 2,000 applicants on the basis of their shooting and riding skills and on their abilities as engineers, miners, farmers, butchers, and bakers. Impressed by the pockets of good farmland they saw, the temperate climate they experienced, and the fortune in gold and diamonds they believed lay just beneath the soil, the white pioneers settled in.

Rhodes and his British South Africa Company soon evicted the Shona from the land they had farmed for centuries and forced them to work on white-owned farms for subsistence wages. But the Shona lands yielded few crops and no gold, so the settlers turned their attention to the Ndebele lands of the southeast, where 1,500 whites were already enjoying some success panning gold out of the rivers. In 1893, Rhodes's troops attacked the Ndebele, whom they defeated in a short but bloody war. The Ndebele were forced onto tribal reserves where the land was arid and unsuitable for cultivation, their cattle were taken away, and like the Shona they were forced to work on white-owned farms.

By 1896 the Ndebele and the Shona had realized that whatever differences they had between themselves were less important than the threat they faced from Rhodes's British South Africa Company and the white settlers. That year and on into the next the two peoples rose against the whites in the rebellion that is now referred to as the First Chimurenga, for the Shona word that means, roughly, "war of resistance."

The Ndebele were the first to rebel. Taking advantage of the absence of the colony's police force, who were off in South Africa bungling an attempt to overthrow the Afrikaner government, the Ndebele descended on white farms, killing scores of settlers and forcing the white population into forts. Encouraged by the success of the Ndebele, at the start of 1897 the Shona — who the whites had characterized as "cowardly" and "servile" — attacked whites throughout their portion of the country. But by the end of the year Rhodes's troops had put down the revolt, killing several hundred Africans, and asserting their control throughout the country. Nevertheless, Chimurenga I left a lasting impression on the whites of the colony. Almost 400 settlers — 10 percent of the white population — were killed in the rebellion. The whites would never forget the ferocity of the African uprising, and over the ensuing decades they would do everything they could to prevent it from happening again.

Zimbabwe was now called Rhodesia in honor of Rhodes. The British South Africa Company established a central government, making Rhodesia (or Southern Rhodesia, as it was officially known) a full-fledged British colony. To the north lay two more areas under the company's administration, Nyasaland and Northern Rhodesia, neither of which had a significant number of white settlers.

The British South Africa Company governed Rhodesia until 1923, when the company's charter expired and the colony's white male adults voted in a referendum to choose between self-government or union with South Africa. Fifty-nine percent of the 15,000 voters chose self-government, and the British accordingly allowed the white settlers to elect a parliament and prime minister. The British government retained the right to veto any legislation by the settlers that it considered discriminatory against the country's black population, but it would never use this power, even though most of the legislation passed by the settlers was blatantly discriminatory.

The black African population of Rhodesia, which made up the vast majority of the country's inhabitants, suffered severely under white European rule. For example, by 1900, just 10 years after they had arrived, the handful of white settlers had taken for themselves 1/6 of Rhodesia's land — and the percentage rose steadily as the years went by. The white settlers simply evicted blacks from huge tracts of land, which they then claimed belonged legally to the whites. The only places where blacks were allowed to own and farm land were on overcrowded tribal reserves.

Cecil Rhodes was the founder of the British South Africa Company (BSA), the mining corporation that occupied and colonized Rhodesia. A firm believer in the superiority of the white, English-speaking peoples, he also founded the Rhodes scholarships, to instill "moral force of character" in future leaders.

A group of Ndebele soldiers during the First Chimurenga of 1896—97, the unsuccessful Ndebele and Shona rebellion against the white settlers. Some 400 whites — 10 percent of the settlers — were killed during the rebellion, but Rhodes's soldiers killed thousands of blacks before he personally negotiated an end to the fighting in 1897.

The soil was usually poor within the reserves, which were a long distance from markets where crops could be exchanged for necessities. The 34,000 Rhodesian whites kept for themselves the land on which there were towns, industrial areas, roads, railroads, and good soil. They hired blacks to farm the land for them, but paid them barely enough to live on. Ironically, malnourishment became a serious problem for many blacks working to harvest the bountiful yields on large, flourishing, white-owned farms.

Some of the blacks whose land was taken were forced to labor in the company mines, often at low wages for more than 10 hours at a time. Other blacks went to the cities to work at subsistence wages in factories and as domestic servants. Qualified blacks were not permitted to take certain skilled jobs, which were reserved for whites; when they held the same jobs as whites, they were paid much lower wages.

Meanwhile, the settler government deprived Africans of most of their political rights. It was difficult for Africans to form trade unions, almost impossible for them to strike legally, and they were barred from living in white neighborhoods. Although blacks were forced to pay taxes to the settler government, they did not receive equal benefits. The colonial government spent up to 10 times as much for a white child in school as it did for a black schoolchild, and white parents, who earned on average 11 times more than black parents, had to pay less in school fees for their children than black parents did. Many black parents could not afford to send their children to school and in many rural areas black children were educated only if there was a missionary school.

The new, self-governing colony was building a structure of systematic, legally enforced racism, designed to keep the black majority a cheap labor force, impoverished, uneducated, and unable to overthrow the white minority. For blacks, who had already suffered greatly in the initial white conquest of the country in the 1890s, the situation was only getting worse.

It was into these circumstances that Robert Gabriel Mugabe was born, to a peasant family on February 21, 1924, near the Kutama Catholic mission. He was a Zezuru, one of the clans that make up the Shona people. Robert's mother, Bona, raised her four sons, Miteri, Raphael, Robert, Dhonandho, and one daughter, Sabina, by herself. She taught catechism for a living but her salary was meager,

A black man being flogged by BSA officers in the 1890s. The first white settlers occupied Shona lands, then Ndebele lands, in both cases forcing the Africans to live on arid tribal reserves. The entire effort was directed by the BSA's private army; the colony's government and courts were also run by the company.

so from a very young age, Robert helped raise money for the family by tending cattle for his grandfather and fishing. Robert's father, Gabriel Mugabe, left the family to work in the South African mines when Robert was 10. He rarely sent money and eventually disappeared.

When Robert was young, the Kutama mission was run by Father Loubiére, a strict French priest who had little respect for traditional African ways. He made all the women of the mission wear long dresses that covered every inch of their body, even though cloth was expensive and the summer heat stifling. Traditionally respected people in African culture, such as healers and spirit mediums, and those who believed in such practices, were forced either to convert to Christianity or to leave the community. Mugabe remembers being invited to the house of a visiting white missionary, and as he left, seeing the missionary carefully wipe off the seats his guests had used.

A BSA guard stands before the workers of a gold-mining compound in northeastern Rhodesia in 1898. Because most productive agricultural lands were reserved for white use, many blacks abandoned farming and were forced to work long hours at low wages in white-owned mines.

When Robert reached the age of six, a new priest arrived to take charge of Kutama mission. His name was Father O'Hea, a Jesuit who believed that all people were equal whatever their race and that the black children near his mission should have as much chance for education as any white child in the country. When O'Hea came to the mission, there was only a primary school, but soon he added a teacher-training school, a technical school, and a hospital. He did so without the help of the Rhodesian government, whose governor tried to dissuade him from raising money for the projects by remarking, "Why do you worry about a hospital — after all, there are too many natives in the country already."

Mugabe was one of Father O'Hea's favorite pupils. O'Hea later said he saw in him "an exceptional mind and an exceptional heart." Mugabe, who grew up speaking both English — used widely among Rhodesian blacks — and Shona, was reported to have had an IQ of 160. He loved school and soon was two grades ahead of his classmates. O'Hea urged Mugabe's mother to let Robert train as a teacher, and although the family had little money, she agreed. O'Hea paid part of the cost, and Robert's grandfather the rest.

A mission school in the 1920s. Mugabe was born at the Jesuit Kutama Mission in 1924, one year after the BSA relinquished power to a government elected by Rhodesia's adult white males. Mugabe was deeply influenced by Christian teachings, but like most of the country's blacks did not practice the religion.

31

Mohandas K. Gandhi, the Indian independence leader who spent many years as an activist in South Africa. His tactic of achieving political change through nonviolence was adopted by South African blacks in the 1940s and later by Rhodesian blacks, but they eventually abandoned it in the face of increasing white intransigence.

Mugabe excelled in the teacher-training course, and when he graduated at the age of 20, he moved on to teach in schools throughout Rhodesia. He spent only a few terms at each school, for he wanted to meet as many new people and learn as much as he could.

There were very few blacks in Rhodesia who were able to finish secondary school and find the money to go to college. So in 1949, when Mugabe won a scholarship to attend Fort Hare University in South Africa, he eagerly accepted. South Africa, like Rhodesia, was governed by a racist white minority. It had separate schools for blacks and whites, reflecting the South African government's obsession with segregating the races. Fort Hare was for blacks only and therefore poorly funded, but it was a good school nonetheless, staffed by the best black teachers available and drawing the brightest pupils from all over southern Africa. Mugabe's ambition when he left for Fort Hare was to become a professor and teach in Rhodesia's black secondary schools. But he would find that his experiences in South Africa were to irrevocably change the course of his life.

Mugabe found Fort Hare University in the midst of great political ferment and his exposure to the debates going on there would provide the foundations for his own political philosophy. In 1947, India, Britain's largest and most profitable colony, had gained its independence, largely through the campaign of nonviolent resistance led by Mohandas K. Gandhi. Gandhi was assassinated one year after India became independent and one year before Mugabe arrived in Fort Hare, and his teachings were still widely influential. Gandhi spent nearly 20 years in South Africa, where as a young man he campaigned for the rights of Indians, blacks, and people of mixed race. Thus his political philosophy and achievements were a particularly significant subject in that country.

As Mugabe arrived at Fort Hare, the youth wing of the African National Congress (ANC), an organization campaigning for the restoration of rights to South Africa's blacks, was planning a Gandhian campaign of nonviolent resistance to induce the white minority government to allow blacks to vote. Mugabe listened to the organizers of the ANC campaign, Nelson Mandela, Oliver Tambo, and Robert Sobukwe, and decided that Rhodesia too could begin to confront its white settler government and demand black majority rule.

Mugabe was also influenced by the white communists who attended meetings on black nationalism. They encouraged him to read the works of Karl Marx — the 19th-century political philosopher and economist who developed the theories of communism and socialism — and to connect them to his own experiences and those of the black majority in Rhodesia.

When Mugabe studied Marxism with the communists, many of whom were Jewish, he decided that many of the principles of Marxism and Judeo-Christian religion were the same. Noting that his childhood community at the Kutama mission — with its emphasis on sharing and mutual help — strongly resembled a socialist society, Mugabe came to believe that socialism was "much more Christian than capitalism," as he later put it. It was a belief buttressed by Mugabe's experience of capitalism: the virtual enslavement of blacks by Rhodesian whites so that the whites could make the greatest possible profits in farming, mining, and other business enterprises.

"Christian principles which have become part of our society," Mugabe would tell a Nigerian interviewer more than 30 years later, "[such as] loving your neighbour and doing unto others as you would want others to do unto you. . . . I think those are consonant with Marxism, with the basic spirit of Marxism. In fact Christianity and Marxism should be in love with each other. Unfortunately, they are at war with each other. But one would want to see them reconciled in our own society."

Mugabe joined the ANC before he left South Africa with his bachelor of arts degree and his diploma in education. He resolved to bring the struggle for majority rule to Rhodesia but was not yet certain how

> *I felt already that I was a revolutionary.*
> —ROBERT MUGABE
> reflecting on his experiences as a student at Fort Hare University

to organize such a movement. After he taught for a few years in mission schools in Rhodesia, he spent many years traveling to other African countries to teach, study, and learn from the people he met. In 1955 he went to Northern Rhodesia to study for a graduate degree.

Two years earlier Northern Rhodesia and Nyasaland had joined Rhodesia in a federation, an arrangement the 3 white-ruled British colonies would maintain for the next 11 years. In none of the three countries were blacks consulted on the federation plan, and they deeply resented their exclusion from the process. Thus the brief federation spurred the creation of what was then Rhodesia's largest black-rights movement ever, the City Youth League, in 1956. Mugabe arrived in Northern Rhodesia in time to witness this first small step in the development of a permanent black political organization.

In 1957 Mugabe went to Ghana to further his studies, and it was there that he found proof that an independent black-ruled nation was an attainable dream. In that year, Ghana, which had been a British possession, became the first colony in black Africa to achieve independence. Its new leader,

The graduating class of 1951 at South Africa's Fort Hare University, where Mugabe was studying at the time. It was at this black university that Mugabe embraced Marxism and became involved in the South African black majority's struggle for rights against that country's white racist regime.

Kwame Nkrumah, invited educated Africans to come to Ghana and help make the country one that all of Africa still under colonial rule could be proud of — and one that would inspire respect in Europeans and North Americans, so many of whom belittled black Africans as ignorant and incapable of governing themselves. Ghana's president, cabinet ministers, educators, and businesspeople were black, and the continent followed its progress with pride and enthusiasm. If this could happen in Ghana, Mugabe realized, it could happen in Rhodesia too.

In Ghana, Mugabe met Sally Heyfron, an instructor at a local college. She came from an educated middle-class black family; her father was also a teacher, and her mother a magistrate. One day Mugabe burned himself so badly that he was sent to the hospital. Heyfron knew he was alone in a strange country, so she visited him often. They became good friends, and Heyfron's family got to know Mugabe well.

In 1960, after three years in Ghana, Robert Mugabe took Sally Heyfron back to Rhodesia with him to get married. She took his name, and together they prepared to become involved in the newly forming Zimbabwean independence movement.

In 1960 Mugabe married Sally Heyfron, the Ghanian daughter of a teacher and a magistrate. Mugabe and Heyfron, who took her husband's last name, had met three years earlier in Ghana, when it became the first colony in black Africa to gain independence.

RHODESIA says YES

ISSUED BY S.A. KOCK Box 3050 SALISBURY. PRINTED BY

3

The Forces Gather

Mugabe returned to Rhodesia in time to participate in a march organized to protest the arrest of the leaders of the National Democratic party (NDP), an organization calling for majority rule. On July 20, 1960, more than half the African workers in Salisbury, Rhodesia's capital and largest city, left their jobs to participate in the march. One of Mugabe's friends asked him to address the 25,000 marchers on his vision of a free Zimbabwe.

Mugabe said that the nationalist movement led by the NDP would succeed only if all classes — workers and peasants as well as the educated and wealthy — participated. According to the Zimbabwean writer Eshmael Mlambo, the crowd was delighted to hear a university graduate who had traveled extensively tell them that freedom could not be won without the poor and illiterate.

More than 4,000 of the marchers stayed together overnight, waiting for the Rhodesian prime minister, Sir Edgar Whitehead, to meet with them and discuss the release of their leaders. But in the morning police fired tear gas into the crowd, chasing the

We are no longer asking Europeans to rule us well. We now want to rule ourselves.
—LEOPOLD TAKAWIRA
speaking at the first
meeting of the NDP

Rhodesian prime minister Sir Edgar Whitehead stands before an election poster in 1961. Whitehead agreed to limited representation for blacks in the Rhodesian parliament and promised to return some lands to blacks — moves that angered conservative whites. He was forced to resign in 1962.

Rhodesian soldiers watch Joshua Nkomo, leader of the National Democratic Party (NDP), in 1961. Nkomo had already headed two other black political parties that were outlawed by the Rhodesian government. In December 1961 the NDP too was banned.

demonstrators back to the poor neighborhoods in and around Salisbury. The marchers set up barricades and stoned police cars. In the week that followed, rioting broke out in which the NDP estimated that 36 Africans were killed. More than 100 people were arrested and many more were hurt, but in the end the protesters had achieved their aim: The NDP leaders were released from prison.

Encouraged, the NDP looked for new ways to challenge the colonial government. In October 1960 the NDP held its first party congress and Mugabe was elected to the post of publicity secretary — not a particularly important job, but Mugabe soon made an impression on the party. He organized an NDP youth wing to encourage younger people to take an active role in the party.

At rallies, Mugabe reminded Africans that they had a proud heritage and civilization of their own. The sights and sounds at NDP meetings were quintessentially African: drums beating, the wearing of national costumes, dancing, and traditional prayers. Mugabe encouraged men to take off their tie, jacket, and shoes to symbolize a rejection of white colonial culture. White members of the NDP would remove their shoes when they spoke at the rallies to symbolize their respect for African traditions.

On January 7, 1961, Joshua Nkomo, just back from exile in Britain, was elected the leader of the NDP. Nkomo, who would later be known by the nickname Father Zimbabwe, was a genial 300-pounder with graying hair and a penchant for speaking bluntly. Nkomo — a Kalanga, one of the Shona clans that had been assimilated into Ndebele culture — had been a leader of the City Youth League when it was founded in 1956. The next year the City Youth League was reorganized as the Rhodesian branch of the African National Congress, and Nkomo became its leader. But in 1959 the Rhodesian ANC was outlawed by the colonial government; Nkomo, facing a possible jail sentence under the Sedition Act, which made it illegal "to engender feelings of hostility between Europeans and others," was forced to flee to London. The Rhodesian ANC had to be reorganized again and became the NDP.

Nkomo returned in early 1961, when Prime Minister Whitehead agreed to hold a conference to discuss how the black majority in the country would be represented in government. Nkomo demanded that at least 25 of the 50 seats in the Rhodesian parliament be set aside for black delegates and that all Africans be permitted to vote in elections for the 25 black seats. The whites wanted to permit only 5 black seats and to allow only educated and wealthy blacks to vote for these few delegates. Eventually Whitehead offered to set aside 15 seats in parliament for blacks.

Nkomo agreed to the 15 seats — which gave the 95-percent black majority just 30-percent representation in parliament — and called it an acceptable compromise. The rest of the NDP leadership, though, was furious at Nkomo's decision; Mugabe, for example, called Nkomo's agreement a sellout. Members of the NDP were so unhappy with the results of the constitutional conference that they held a referendum of their members: Should the NDP accept the constitution and let NDP candidates compete for those 15 seats? Political meetings were illegal, but Mugabe got around the ban by holding the meetings in open fields and on buses that carried blacks to their jobs. Members voted their pref-

Mugabe, head of the NDP youth wing, addressing a party rally in 1961. The NDP called for strikes and other nonviolent actions to protest the government's racist policies. It also advocated the establishment of a one-person, one-vote electoral system, regardless of race — a scheme that would have meant the end of white rule.

erence and dispersed before the police got wind of the meeting. Eventually the party leadership announced that NDP members voted 372,546 to 471 to reject the constitution and boycott the elections.

The NDP asked its female members to organize a mass demonstration to protest the proposed constitution and the harassment of NDP leaders. More than 10,000 women, many carrying children on their back, marched through Salisbury to protest. Police, using dogs, attacked the women and made 2,000 arrests. The women refused to pay fines levied against them by the courts.

Mugabe suggested that the next move in the campaign of passive resistance might be to boycott work. "If European industries are used to buy guns which are aimed at us," he said, "we must withdraw our labour and our custom and destroy those industries." But before a boycott could get under way, the government banned the NDP, on December 9, 1961.

A policeman restrains a demonstrator in 1963. To replace the banned NDP, Nkomo formed the Zimbabwe African People's Union (ZAPU), which was in turn outlawed by the Rhodesian government in 1962. Over the next year demonstrations and riots in support of ZAPU rocked the country, and scores were killed by the police.

A few days later Nkomo and the NDP leadership, including Mugabe, got around the ban by reorganizing the party under a new name, the Zimbabwe African People's Union (ZAPU). ZAPU, like the NDP, stated that it had no objection to allowing the white settlers to remain in the country; it just wanted blacks and whites to be treated as equals under the law, with each person entitled to one vote regardless of color or the level of education or income.

Tens of thousands of people came to ZAPU gatherings to listen to their nationalist leaders, despite the efforts of the white police to break up the rallies, often with guns and tear gas. Several blacks were killed and many more injured as the result of police actions at early ZAPU rallies.

In 1962, with many countries in Africa becoming independent and more scheduled to become independent within a few years, many Rhodesians thought their nation would soon gain independence from Britain. Some moderate whites and many blacks predicted that Nkomo, boosted by his position as leader of ZAPU, would be elected the country's first prime minister upon independence. White businesspeople consulted with ZAPU to learn what economic policies it planned to introduce at independence and many moderate whites began to join the party. Conservative whites, fearing ZAPU's strength, convinced Prime Minister Whitehead to ban it on September 19, 1962.

In 1963 most ZAPU officials, including Mugabe, fled Rhodesia. A split soon developed between Nkomo and several ZAPU leaders, who in 1963 formed a new party, the Zimbabwe African National Union (ZANU). This photo includes ZANU head Ndabaningi Sithole (fourth from right) and Mugabe (third from right).

Guerrillas training in Tanzania in the mid-1960s. Late in 1963 Mugabe, Sithole, Nkomo, and most other black leaders were arrested by the Rhodesian government. While in prison, the ZANU leadership decided to begin a guerrilla war against the white regime. The first attack occurred in 1964.

Frustrated by the government's repeated crackdowns against conventional political protest and aware that Africans in other colonies had to resort to warfare before they were promised independence by their respective colonial governments, the ZAPU leadership began to consider using violent means to bring about change.

A few days after the party was outlawed, ZAPU and its supporters reacted with a wave of violence that included rioting, the burning of government buildings, and gasoline-bomb attacks on white farms. Police rounded up and beat hundreds of people they suspected of being ZAPU sympathizers. Some 1,600 blacks were arrested, including Mugabe, who was restricted to a mud hut with a tin roof in a tribal reserve for several months. Nkomo was out of the country when the arrests took place and tried to persuade the rest of the ZAPU leadership to join him in exile. But they remained in Rhodesia, preferring to stay close to their followers, and convinced Nkomo to return and serve out his restriction period with the other ZAPU leaders.

Meanwhile, white Rhodesians had become disenchanted with Whitehead and his United Federal party. His overtures to the black leadership in 1961, his 1962 pledge to bring about a more equitable land distribution between the races, and the September riots resulted in the white electorate voting him out of office in December 1962. The new prime minister was Winston Field of the conservative Rhodesian Front party. As the restriction orders against the ZAPU leadership expired, Field and the Rhodesian Front started to push through new, even more discriminatory legislation against blacks.

One of the first new laws passed by the Rhodesian Front was an act enforcing a mandatory death sentence against anyone convicted of sabotage. Robert Mugabe called the sabotage act "legislation for murder" and characterized the Rhodesian Front as "a bunch of cowboys." Sally Mugabe criticized the British government, under the ceremonial leadership of Queen Elizabeth II, for doing nothing to stop the repressive legislation. "The Queen can go to hell," she said. Both were charged with subversion.

Nkomo too, just back from a visit with President Julius Nyerere of Tanzania, faced charges for holding political meetings, illegal for blacks. While out on bail, Nkomo once again tried to persuade the banned ZAPU leadership to go into exile, and again the other leaders resisted, believing that they must be willing to risk jail sentences and undergo the same hardships as the rest of the nation's blacks.

Nkomo told them that Nyerere and Kenneth Kaunda — the black leader of Northern Rhodesia, which under the name of Zambia was about to be granted independence by Britain — had advised

South African prime minister John Vorster expresses his support for UDI and Rhodesian prime minister Ian Smith (left) late in 1965, after the United Nations imposed a trade embargo on Rhodesia. ZANU and ZAPU guerrillas increased their operations in response to UDI, prompting South Africa to aid Rhodesia's white regime.

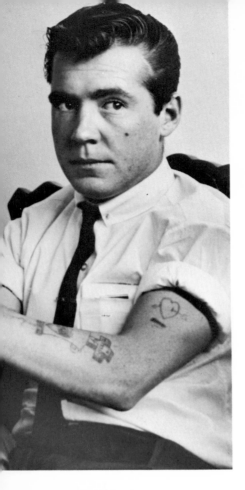

A prospective mercenary awaits an interview in Rhodesia in the mid-1960s. With blacks outnumbering whites 20 to 1, the government hired hundreds of foreign mercenaries throughout the 1960s and 1970s to join the Rhodesian army in its war against the Zimbabwean guerrillas.

them to go into exile. Mugabe and several others still did not want to leave, but they respected Nyerere and Kaunda and agreed to follow their advice. Robert and Sally Mugabe jumped bail and with the rest of the ZAPU leadership traveled to Tanzania, where they learned that Nyerere had never told Nkomo that they should seek exile. Nyerere did not want the level of his country's involvement in the Zimbabwean liberation struggle to be high enough to draw a Rhodesian military response; he believed the ZAPU leaders should have stayed in Rhodesia. Kaunda wrote them a letter giving the same advice.

Mugabe and the others were furious with Nkomo. When the ZAPU leadership attended the conference of the Organization of African Unity (OAU), which included the governments of all the independent African countries, they learned that the OAU's advice was also to return home and fight from within the country.

The ZAPU leadership sent a letter to party members saying they planned to discuss removing Nkomo from power. Nkomo took the initiative and suspended four members of the leadership, including Mugabe. Nkomo then had himself elected "president for life" of ZAPU — with the power to appoint and dismiss party leaders without consulting ZAPU members—and returned to Rhodesia.

The members still in Tanzania met and decided to form a new party, the Zimbabwe African National Union (ZANU), to be led by Ndabaningi Sithole, another nationalist leader who had been suspended by Nkomo. ZANU's members were predominantly Shona, while most Ndebele remained with Nkomo's ZAPU. Shortly after ZANU was formed, rioting between Nkomo supporters and ZANU supporters broke out in several areas of Rhodesia, killing dozens of people.

Mugabe put off returning to Rhodesia to begin his prison sentence. The Mugabes had lost a child at birth one year before and now Sally Mugabe was pregnant again. The pregnancy had been difficult; if she returned to Rhodesia with Robert, she would be sent to prison and would almost certainly lose the baby under the harsh prison conditions. But in

August their son, Nhamodzenyika, was born; the name meant "suffering country" in the Shona language.

In December 1963, Sally and Nhamodzenyika left for Ghana to live with her parents, and Robert returned to Rhodesia to begin his jail term. He would serve nine months before being released. While serving the term, the events leading to the outbreak of the long war of liberation would come to a head.

In 1964, Zambia, formerly Northern Rhodesia, and Malawi, formerly Nyasaland, were granted their independence by Britain, cementing the resolve of Rhodesian blacks to fight for their own independence. The installation of black rule in Rhodesia's neighbors and former partners in federation also prompted the white Rhodesian government to react still more harshly to black nationalist activity.

That same year, the British government demanded that Rhodesia prepare for black majority rule as a precondition to granting the country independence. Rhodesian whites, outraged, urged Prime Minister Field to preserve white rule by declaring independence without Britain's permission. Field balked and was forced to resign by his own party. Ian Smith took over the prime ministership and called a referendum in which all Rhodesian whites would vote on whether the country should declare the Unilateral Declaration of Independence. They did, and when the results were in they had approved UDI by a 10-to-1 margin.

ZANU met to discuss what it would do in the face of the whites' intransigence and decided to begin the fighting. Smith banned the party and ordered the arrest of its leaders. It was at this point that the fighting broke out. A small detachment of ZANU guerrilla fighters killed a local Rhodesian Front party official, the first time since 1897 that a white Rhodesian had been killed by blacks in an act of war.

The ZANU guerrillas had undergone several months' training in China, whose communist government regularly aided independence movements around the world. Chinese advisers would continue to train ZANU soldiers over the course of the conflict,

This fascist settler cowboy government is preparing to unilaterally declare Rhodesia independent from Britain for the settlers to subject millions of Africans to slavery.
—ROBERT MUGABE
on the Rhodesian government's plans for the future

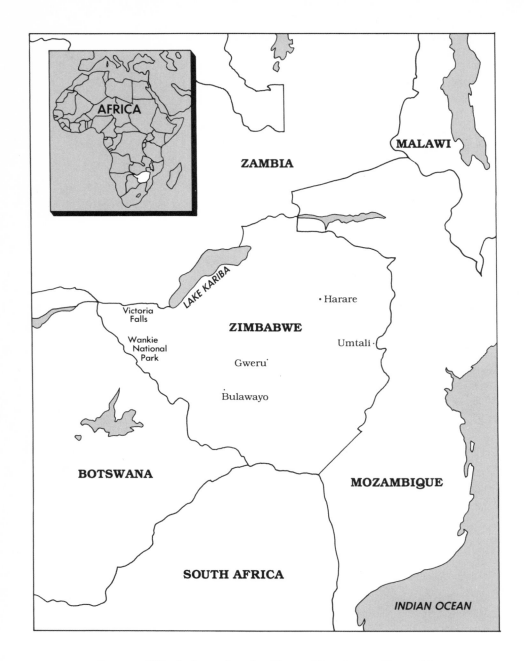

A map of Zimbabwe showing its position in southern Africa. Until 1964, Zambia and Malawi were the British colonies of Northern Rhodesia and Nyasaland; Zimbabwe was known as Rhodesia until 1980, and Harare was called Salisbury until 1982.

as ZANU increasingly became identified as a Marxist organization. Nkomo's ZAPU sent its first guerrillas into action in 1965, and it would receive most of its aid from the Soviet Union.

In the first couple of years of the war, the guerrillas, short of recruits, actually pressed scores of young men into service against their will, through abduction or the threat of physical violence. This method of conscription was stopped when the level of desertion proved too high. Once enlistment became purely voluntary, the number of recruits rose slowly through the late 1960s and much more rapidly with the start of the 1970s. Soon black Zimbabweans spoke with pride about the young men of their villages who had gone into the bush to fight with the guerrillas. They called the fighters *vakomana*—literally, "the boys."

In November 1965 Ian Smith signed the UDI, and the Rhodesian government's military response began in earnest. Mugabe and Nkomo were put into detention in 1963; Mugabe would remain there for 11 years, Nkomo for 10, and many more black leaders were held for similar lengths of time. Conditions in jails and detention camps like Sikombela were harsh, but Mugabe made the most of them, teaching, studying, organizing, and trying to stay in touch with the slowly but steadily escalating guerrilla war being waged by ZANU troops against Smith's UDI government.

The ZANU guerrillas were accompanied into battle by fighters from the ANC, the black South African liberation organization. ANC guerrillas and saboteurs had been able to do little within South Africa and saw a greater opportunity for success in Rhodesia, South Africa's neighbor and closest ally. By 1967, though, the ANC's alliance with ZANU would cause South Africa to send 2,000 paramilitary police to Rhodesia to fight alongside the forces of the UDI regime.

In 1968 the United Nations passed a resolution banning its members from conducting trade with Rhodesia. Although Rhodesian industry rebounded remarkably well by producing many goods that had

> *You [the British] are going away, leaving Africans in the hands of these people here. Which to you is the greater moral issue? To leave us at the mercy of these people here and in danger, or to use force, shed some blood but put things right? Remember these Europeans could do anything with the African people here— They could use military force, detain them all.*
> —LEOPOLD TAKAWIRA
> on Britain's passive
> acceptance of Smith's UDI

previously been imported, it was nevertheless a major blow against the government. South Africa stepped in to supply Rhodesia with arms and industrial goods in addition to the paramilitary troops it had already sent into the fighting.

Meanwhile, the imprisoned Mugabe learned that Nhamodzenyika had died of encephalitis in Ghana. Heartbroken, he begged the governor to release him from prison long enough to be with Sally for the burial of their son. The governor refused.

After Nhamodzenyika's death, Sally Mugabe went to London, where she studied for a degree in home economics at the University of London. When she was not busy studying or rallying support for ZANU, she helped Robert earn his law degree by copying whole textbooks in longhand and sending them as letters.

In 1969, ZANU leader Ndabaningi Sithole made an error that would cost him the leadership of the independence movement. While he was in detention, a letter bearing his signature on how Prime Minister Ian Smith could be assassinated was smuggled out in a crate of oranges. The letter was found by Rhodesian security officers and Sithole was brought into court to stand trial. During the proceedings Sithole denied writing the letter and pleaded innocent, but after he was found guilty and sentenced to six years' imprisonment he renounced violence and any challenge to the Smith government. He later suggested to ZANU's other members that they dissolve the party and renounce its aims so that they might be freed from detention. Outraged at Sithole for what they believed was a betrayal, the other ZANU members in detention censured him. Finally, in 1974, they would suspend him outright and name Mugabe acting leader of ZANU.

In 1972 Mugabe learned that a group of ZANU guerrillas had killed four Rhodesian soldiers. This was ZANU's most serious attack on the Rhodesian army; soon ZANU and ZAPU guerrilla forces began to mount larger and more frequent attacks while the Rhodesian military responded with increasingly greater firepower. Then, in April 1974, Portugal's military dictatorship was ousted in a bloodless revolution, and the new socialist government promised to grant independence to Mozambique and Portugal's other African colonies, whose black populations had been fighting guerrilla wars against Portuguese colonial rule for years.

At this point the South African government realized that the sort of violence that had brought Mozambique the promise of independence might soon take place in Rhodesia — and from there spread to white-minority-ruled South Africa. South African prime minister John Vorster persuaded Ian Smith to reach a settlement with Rhodesia's African nationalist parties. The negotiations were to be held in Lusaka, the capital of Zambia, and would involve all of Rhodesia's black leaders. Smith ordered the release of Mugabe and Nkomo and flew them to Lusaka to participate in the talks.

In Lusaka, Robert Mugabe saw Sally for the first time in more than a decade, but the talks were a total failure. Smith entered the negotiations certain that they would lead to nothing. "If you can achieve unity," he told his negotiating team, waving his hand, "you can come back and cut this finger off." For his part, Mugabe later said that he participated in the negotiations "purely as a tactic to buy the time we needed to organize and intensify the armed struggle."

Mugabe left the Lusaka talks soon after they began. He returned to Rhodesia to prepare for the next stage of his role in the liberation struggle: to join ZANU's troops in the fighting itself.

[Sithole] was caught in the act of throwing instructions encased in oranges over the prison wall to members of his party. The fruit has been cut out and expertly stuffed with instructions on how Prime Minister Smith was to be assassinated.
—REV. BILL CARK
then chaplain general to all prisons in Rhodesia

4

Chimurenga II

Soon after he dropped out of the Lusaka talks and returned to Rhodesia, Mugabe left the country with hundreds of ZANU followers and walked for several days until they had crossed the eastern border into Mozambique. Mozambique was not yet independent, but large areas of the country were controlled by Mozambican guerrillas who for a dozen years had been fighting the Portuguese colonial government. It was there that ZANU found refuge.

The army of the Mozambican liberation movement, the Mozambique Liberation Front (known by its Portuguese acronym, FRELIMO), had fought so effectively that 40,000 Portuguese soldiers were sent to the colony to try to defeat the revolt in 1973. Throughout the early 1970s, the Portuguese army's efforts to crush FRELIMO had been secretly aided by Rhodesian and South African troops: Both governments wanted to see the white Portuguese minority remain in power so that it could prevent Mozambique from becoming a staging area for guerrilla attacks against Rhodesia and South Africa. FRELIMO in turn joined ZANU's forces in the fighting inside Rhodesia.

They couldn't go freely, they had to escape. In the end they literally walked out of Rhodesia.
—DAVID SMITH
Mugabe biographer, on how Mugabe and his followers left Rhodesia for Mozambique

Robert Mugabe in 1974, after his release from 11 years' imprisonment in Rhodesian jails and detention camps. Mugabe was freed to take part in talks with the Rhodesian government, but soon dropped out of the conference to lead the ZANU forces in the escalating war against the white minority regime.

Mozambican president Samora Machel in uniform in 1980, five years after he led his country to independence. In the 1970s Mugabe looked for guidance to Machel, a committed Marxist and leader of FRELIMO forces. FRELIMO became ZANU's closest ally during the war against the white Rhodesian regime.

FRELIMO finally won the war in 1974, when leftist army officers overthrew Portugal's dictator in a bloodless coup. The new socialist government, citing the military and moral futility of Portugal's policy in Mozambique and its other African colonies, immediately announced that it would withdraw its troops.

When Mugabe arrived in Mozambique in the latter portion of 1974, the cease-fire was in effect in that country; the new Portuguese government had already agreed to grant Mozambique independence and transfer power to FRELIMO. FRELIMO was a Marxist organization led by Samora Machel, a 41-year-old former nurse who had served as a guerrilla leader since 1963 and the organization's political and military head since 1970. Already recognized as one of black Africa's most capable leaders, Machel would go on to play a towering role not only in Mozambican and southern African affairs, but as a personal influence on Mugabe himself.

ZANU arrived in Mozambique in disarray. Although the ZANU members who had been jailed with Sithole no longer recognized him as the organization's leader, there had been no public announcement that he had been replaced by Mugabe. Sithole, still claiming to be ZANU's president, was participating in the continuing Lusaka negotiations with Smith, Nkomo, and another prominent Rhodesian black, Bishop Abel Muzorewa.

Not only was the situation within the ZANU power structure confused, but the organization's fighters were also in some difficulty. FRELIMO had been training ZANU soldiers since 1970, but the bulk of both ZANU's and ZAPU's guerrilla forces had been based in Zambia, which made it the frequent target of Rhodesian military attacks. In March 1975 Herbert Chitepo, a high-ranking ZANU leader, was killed in Zambia by unknown assassins in a car-bomb explosion. Following the assassination, ZANU leaders were arrested throughout Rhodesia — and more surprisingly, throughout Zambia, making it obvious that ZANU forces would have to be based in some other place. With Mozambique about to come under Marxist and black majority rule, ZANU prepared to move most of its operations there.

Within 6 months of Mugabe's arrival in Mozambique, some 10,000 men, women, and children followed. In a public memorandum, 44 commanders of ZANU's guerrilla army criticized Nkomo, Sithole, and Muzorewa for continuing to talk to the Rhodesian government. They announced that Mugabe was the only person they would accept as their political leader.

When the Lusaka talks finally collapsed in 1975, Nkomo decided to rejoin Mugabe in the guerrilla war against the Rhodesian government. ZANU and Nkomo's ZAPU formed a joint force in Mozambique, with a military wing called the Zimbabwe People's Army and later a political wing called the Patriotic Front. In 1976 the Zimbabwe People's Army staged a major attack on several white farms, and although the guerrillas suffered more heavily than the Rhodesian army, the Smith regime was shaken. A new stage in the war had clearly begun.

Smith increased the troop strength of the security forces from 21,000 to 35,000 and ordered attacks on guerrilla camps in Mozambique. The raids resulted in the massacre of hundreds of people, most of them unarmed civilians. The United Nations condemned the raids and Machel, now the president of Mozambique, responded by closing the border with Rhodesia. The Rhodesian government called the victims of the attacks "terrorists" and maintained that the deaths of civilians killed in the raids were regrettable but inevitable, as they were being trained to become guerrillas. Throughout the war Rhodesian attacks against Mozambique, Zambia, and Botswana would exact a heavy toll on those nations for their support of the Zimbabwean guerrillas. The three countries, as well as Tanzania, would become known as the frontline states for hosting the guerrillas and thus making themselves targets for Rhodesian raids.

The alliance between ZANU and ZAPU was uneasy, not just because one was predominantly Shona and the other Ndebele, but also because Nkomo continued to carry on negotiations with Smith in an effort to reach a diplomatic solution, despite the objections of Mugabe and Machel. Meanwhile, ZAPU soldiers were unwilling to enter combat

Guerrillas from the Mozambican Liberation Front (FRELIMO) in the early 1970s. After a decade of fighting against Portuguese white colonial forces, FRELIMO controlled large portions of Mozambique along the Rhodesian border. ZANU set up guerrilla bases there; Nkomo and the ZAPU forces were based in Botswana.

Members of a Rhodesian infantry unit taking a villager for questioning. Although the Rhodesian army gained worldwide admiration among military experts for its effectiveness, much of its strategy involved the indiscriminate massacre of civilians, terror bombings, and even the poisoning of supplies for refugee camps.

while their leader was negotiating with Smith. ZANU guerrillas resented the fact that they were doing most of the fighting.

ZANU developed a three-stage military strategy that relied heavily on the support of Rhodesia's black peasant farmers. First, ZANU political officers taught local peasants about ZANU's aims and encouraged the peasants to participate in the organization's political meetings. Second, with these sympathetic peasants to protect and assist them, ZANU fighters would use the farms as supply and staging areas to mount guerrilla attacks against government forces. Finally, if ZANU succeeded in securing a region, it would set up a provisional government that ensured peasant participation, and use the liberated zone as a base from which to move into neighboring areas. The strategy was based on the successful one used in the communist revolution in China, where a substantial number of ZANU's military leaders were trained.

Reliance on women as guerrillas was a policy common to both ZANU and ZAPU. Approximately 15 percent of the ZANU and ZAPU soldiers engaged in combat were women, and another 10 percent performed the dangerous job of transporting arms and materials to the guerrilla camps. Many more women worked at the main bases inside Mozambique or taught civilians inside Rhodesia about gathering intelligence and how to hide supplies, ammunition, and wounded soldiers.

The participation of women in warfare was a Zimbabwean tradition at least as old as Chimurenga I, in which one of the major figures was an old woman named Nehanda Nyakasikana. She was a spirit medium — in Shona belief, an intermediary between the living and the spirits of dead ancestors — who acted as a battlefield commander for the African forces before she was captured and hanged by the white authorities. In 1972, an old woman who was thought to be the medium for Nehanda was brought to a guerrilla camp on the northern frontier to inspire the troops.

One of the ZANU guerrillas' new recruits in 1973 was an 18-year-old woman named Teurai Ropa

Nhongo. In 1974 she became political commissar in charge of one of the camps in Mozambique, director of politics in another camp in 1976, and by 1977 was elected to the highest policy-making body of ZANU, the central committee. In 1981 she described the conditions for the soldiers, both men and women, in Mozambique during the war:

> It is difficult for most people to believe what it was like. In war we ate worms, baboons, tortoises, and dogs, drank urine, and cooked any leaf we could find because there was nothing else. In one camp — it was a refugee camp of women and children refugees, but it was badly bombed — we used to bury 30 people a day; if there were less we would pray and thank God.

The Zimbabwe People's Army eventually broke up into its two factions, ZANU and ZAPU, and after another unsuccessful attempt to negotiate with the Smith government in 1976, ZAPU's army began fighting out of Botswana while ZANU's army continued to fight from Mozambique. Some of the money for weapons and for the refugee camps in Mozambique came from Sally Mugabe, who toured Scandinavia to raise funds.

The fighting was arduous and costly. The Rhodesian army was a small but efficient one, well-equipped with sophisticated weaponry supplied by South Africa and favoring swift, small-scale attacks against the guerrillas. It inflicted enormous losses on ZANU and ZAPU forces while taking few casualties itself — a necessity in light of the small size of the white Rhodesian community. The Rhodesian government forces, however, could by no means be called a "white army"; though it was commanded by whites, the majority of its soldiers were black Rhodesians.

Elite Rhodesian army units such as the Selous Scouts — named after Frederick Selous, the hunter who helped lead the original white pioneer column that occupied the country in 1890 — and the Grey's Scouts cavalry, soon became world famous for the effectiveness of their counterinsurgency techniques. But it was not enough. As the war escalated, white civilian farmers and city dwellers began to

Zimbabwean women undergoing guerrilla training at a ZANU base in Mozambique. Although women held few positions of leadership in ZANU and ZAPU, they made up as much as 15 percent of the black nationalist fighters in the Second Chimurenga, as the war for black majority rule in Rhodesia was known.

A Rhodesian woman at a firing range during the war. White Rhodesian civilians, especially those living on farms or in rural towns, were under constant threat of guerrilla attack by ZANU and ZAPU forces. By the early 1970s most white civilians carried rifles wherever they went.

carry rifles wherever they went; eventually, even men above the age of 60 were organized into militia units. Through all of this, the besieged white Rhodesian community bore their situation with remarkable good humor. After Umtali, a former tourist spot in the eastern hills, came under a concentrated mortar attack in 1978, local whites started wearing T-shirts that read, Come to Umtali and Get Bombed.

But underlying the resilient good nature of many Rhodesian whites during the war was an unmistakable strain of cruelty. The much-admired counterinsurgency techniques of the Selous Scouts and the rest of the Rhodesian military relied heavily on indiscriminate reprisals against unarmed civilians. Hundreds were massacred in raids on refugee camps in Mozambique, Botswana, and Zambia, and refugees in other camps died when Rhodesian intelligence smuggled poisoned food and clothing in with United Nations relief supplies. Rhodesian intelligence also planted bombs in an assassination campaign against ZANU and ZAPU leaders. Even the colorful Rhodesian military slang — which habitually renamed everything from crocodiles ("flat dogs") to sneakers worn on clandestine missions ("clandies") — often carried more than a hint of cruelty. All civilian and military victims of the Rhodesian army were referred to in official government communiqués as "terrorists," leading the Rhodesian soldiers to call them "ters" for short. Bullets were called "harmony pills." Blacks were called "floppers" for the way they supposedly fell when they were shot.

But the ferocity of the Rhodesian military response, designed to intimidate the nation's blacks from joining the guerrillas, only served to strengthen their resolve. The bombing of villages inside Rhodesia forced tens of thousands of refugees to flee to the surrounding countries, where many joined the liberation movement; by 1978, 150,000 Zimbabwean refugees were living in camps in Mozambique and another 50,000 in Zambia. And despite the appalling conditions in the refugee camps, morale remained high. In 1978 Dr. Dzingai Mutumbuka, who ran ZANU's education program in Mozambique, told the British writers David Martin and Phyllis Johnson about the spirit of the refugee schoolchildren:

> After one Rhodesian attack we didn't have any huts or any cover. Our clothes had been destroyed, our books, everything. I remember one night it was raining non-stop and these kids were lying under trees, drenched, but they were singing, and they kept on singing. They laughed the whole night and they said, "We shall conquer." That kind of spirit could only have been produced by the struggle.

The war dragged on into the late 1970s. Some guerrilla leaders became semilegendary figures under assumed names, which they used instead of their real names in order to avoid government reprisals against their family. Many of these assumed names, called chimurenga names, reflected a certain sense of humor on the part of the guerrillas. One squad leader, a fan of British rock and roll, chose the chimurenga name "Comrade Mick Jagger."

An ad for a firm specializing in reinforcing private vehicles with protective armor, from a 1978 Rhodesian magazine. Although white civilians were often attacked by black nationalist guerrillas, relatively few were killed during the war.

By 1978, ZANU and ZAPU guerrillas had begun winning confrontations with Smith's army. The war was costing the Smith regime up to $1 million a day, and international sanctions imposed against Rhodesia, made worse by the worldwide oil shortage, caused additional economic hardship. Whites were emigrating from Rhodesia at the rate of 1,000 per month. Now leaders of governments throughout the world — not just in southern Africa — began meeting with the Zimbabwean liberation organizations to discuss the future. Victory for the guerrillas was recognized as an inevitability.

In a final attempt to stop the fighting without giving up effective white control of the country, Smith offered what he called the Internal Settlement, in which a black prime minister would be elected and the country would be renamed Zimbabwe Rhodesia — but many top posts, including command of the military, would remain in white hands for an unspecified length of time.

A black policeman stands beside the bodies of seven black nationalist guerrillas in 1977. Many of the soldiers and police in the Rhodesian security forces were black and often fought against ZANU and ZAPU forces. By 1979 a total of 25,000 blacks and 2,000 whites had been killed in 10 years of warfare.

Mugabe and Nkomo rejected the plan as soon as it was offered, saying that the new black prime minister would have no real power. Bishop Abel Muzorewa, a black nationalist leader with some political following but almost no military backing, accepted the settlement and ran for election. So did Ndabaningi Sithole, who had long ago lost his position as leader of ZANU and now led a small splinter group of the party. Muzorewa won the election easily, but international observers were less than convinced of its legitimacy. A British human-rights delegation sent to observe the election called it a "gigantic confidence trick," adding that the electorate was "intimidated in the most callous fashion to vote" in order to make it appear as though the nation's blacks preferred Muzorewa to the absent Mugabe and Nkomo.

In 1978 the war-weary Ian Smith (right) proposed the Internal Settlement, in which he agreed to hand over the prime ministership to whichever black leader won an election sponsored by the Rhodesian government. Mugabe and Nkomo refused to participate, but Bishop Abel Muzorewa (second from left), a moderate, did take part.

Muzorewa supporters celebrate his victory in the Internal Settlement election of May 1979. Muzorewa turned out to be only a figurehead, as Smith and the conservative whites continued to hold the real power. To foster the impression that blacks were duly represented, Rhodesia was renamed Zimbabwe Rhodesia.

THE PRESIDENT OF U.A.N.C.
BISHOP ABEL TENDEKAI MUZOREWA

Muzorewa, who took office as prime minister of Zimbabwe Rhodesia in May 1979, characterized his government as "evolutionary, not revolutionary . . . revolutionary changes would result in absolute chaos." The Muzorewa government did little, however, to promote the evolution of black rights. It failed to institute any programs to accelerate training blacks to take jobs in the government, and almost all of the jobs in the civil service, including secretarial jobs, continued to be held by whites. The first holiday Muzorewa celebrated was in honor of the founder of white Rhodesia, Cecil Rhodes. Muzorewa appointed his brother to two high posts: chairman of a newly formed development company and deputy chairman of another multimillion-dollar corporation. Neither job was publicly advertised to allow other blacks to apply.

Muzorewa had always been extremely critical of the liberation movements that advocated violence in overthrowing the Smith regime and instituting majority rule. For instance, in 1977, before becoming prime minister, Muzorewa helped the Smith government investigate the bombing of a Woolworth's store, charging that the attack was "characteristic of the intimidation and indiscriminate terrorism" of Joshua Nkomo. Nevertheless, in the first 3 months of Muzorewa's term as prime minister, government security forces killed 900 black civilians.

In September 1979, Muzorewa extended martial law to most of the country, giving the military the legal right to burn and bomb villages, and imprison, order into forced labor, or even execute villagers suspected of having assisted Nkomo's and Mugabe's guerrillas. This prompted a black Zimbabwean to sum up his attitude toward Muzorewa for an American newspaper reporter. "The government is so busy trying to reassure the 250,000 whites," he said, "that it has forgotten all about the 7 million blacks in the country." Many tempered their blame for Muzorewa, however, by noting that in reality he had very little power to control the excesses of the Rhodesian military.

Whites retained considerable power in the Internal Settlement government and often seemed to treat Muzorewa as a puppet. For instance, when Ian Smith was prime minister, the supreme commander of the armed forces, General Peter Walls, would come daily to Smith's office to report. But when Muzorewa assumed the prime ministership, he was expected to report each day to Walls's office.

Calling Muzorewa's government a sham, ZANU and ZAPU continued the guerrilla war. Within months, Smith and Muzorewa were forced to concede that the Internal Settlement was a failure. Smith and the whites saw that they would have to relinquish power once and for all.

Blacks in a refugee camp in Zimbabwe Rhodesia. The election of Muzorewa did not stop the fighting between the government and the guerrillas. By 1979, it was estimated that the war had forced one-third of the nation's black population into refugee camps both inside and beyond the borders.

5

From Rhodesia to Zimbabwe

After a long, bloody war that took the lives of 25,000 blacks and 2,000 whites, Ian Smith finally agreed to negotiate a peaceful transfer of power to black majority rule. He had recognized for some time that his ultraconservative white regime, so vastly outnumbered by Rhodesia's blacks and so ostracized by the international community, could not hold out much longer.

Throughout the 1970s, Britain, the United States, and other countries had made several failed attempts to bring the combatants to the negotiating table. But the turning point had come in the summer of 1979, just weeks after Muzorewa had become prime minister of the Internal Settlement government. Margaret Thatcher, the conservative prime minister of Britain, suggested an arrangement that both Smith and the liberation armies considered acceptable. Instead of handing power over to a black majority government themselves, Smith and Muzorewa would dissolve the 15-year Unilateral Declaration of Independence and allow Rhodesia to return to its pre-1965 status as a British colony.

I have no doubt that the Patriotic Front will join the settlement. And I must accept that. There's no point in Smithy staying out in the cold. The referee has blown the whistle, the game's over.
—IAN SMITH

ZANU supporters celebrate Mugabe's landslide election victory on March 4, 1980. His triumph in the election, which was closely monitored by Britain, marked the end of the war and the beginning of black-majority-ruled Zimbabwe, with Mugabe at the helm as prime minister.

A ZAPU soldier hands in his rifle in February 1980 as part of the cease-fire agreement. All ZANU and ZAPU guerrillas convened at assembly points inside the country while government forces were confined to base. The cease-fire was monitored by an 850-man team from Britain, Kenya, Australia, New Zealand, and Fiji.

Britain would then be responsible for negotiating a settlement, drafting a constitution, holding elections, and handing power over to the winner. The British identified four crucial men: Ian Smith, Abel Muzorewa, Joshua Nkomo, and Robert Mugabe, and invited them to a conference organized by British foreign minister Lord Peter Carrington at London's Lancaster House to try to negotiate a settlement.

Mugabe, believing that Thatcher wanted to use the Lancaster House negotiations to justify Britain's recognition of the Muzorewa-Smith government, did not expect them to succeed. Both he and Nkomo hesitated to join the talks, but under pressure from the war-ravaged frontline states they relented and agreed to go to London. When Mugabe arrived at Lancaster House in September 1979, he announced, "We have not come here to negotiate with Smith or Muzorewa. We have not come here to negotiate the principle of majority rule. We have come here to negotiate with the British the transfer of power. Nothing else is for discussion."

The negotiations were dramatic. At one point, one of Mugabe's aides told Prime Minister Thatcher to "jump in the Thames," the river that runs through London; later the usually soft-spoken Mugabe yelled, "Lord Carrington can go to hell!" At no point was anyone, including Mugabe himself, certain about whether he and Smith would agree on a settlement.

Yet, on October 18, 1979, Smith, Muzorewa, Nkomo, and Mugabe all agreed to sign the Lancaster House agreement. The settlement guaranteed whites 20 seats in a new parliament that would have 100 members. The 80 remaining seats would be reserved for blacks. After seven years, the leader of the parliament could decide to abolish the separate white seats and require whites to run in the same elections, for the same seats, as blacks.

Smith and Mugabe both had reservations about the Lancaster House agreement. Smith, although fairly certain that Muzorewa would win the election, felt it gave up too many white privileges; Mugabe doubted that the British would allow ZANU to compete in the election at all.

British prime minister Margaret Thatcher greets delegates in London during the 1979 Lancaster House talks aimed at ending the war between Zimbabwe Rhodesia and the guerrillas. Smith, Muzorewa, Mugabe, and Nkomo all participated in the talks, which resulted in a cease-fire agreement to be followed by free elections.

ZANU(PF) supporters in Salisbury attending the party's first legal political rally, in December 1979. Mugabe was forced to add PF (Patriotic Front) to his party's name because Sithole, leader of a splinter group, had already registered for the election under ZANU.

Lord Carrington, meanwhile, was hailed for bringing about a successful conclusion to the Lancaster House talks. Carrington had mining interests in Rhodesia, South Africa, and in the South African protectorate of Namibia, and dealt extensively with the leaders of the frontline states, who had stressed to him the importance of ending the war.

One year after the talks, the *Times* of London reported that Carrington had had all of the conference chambers and hotel rooms bugged. He was therefore probably aware that the South African government was pressuring Smith to accept the agreement and step down from power. The South Africans were certain that by contributing heavily to Muzorewa's campaign they could guarantee his victory in the election. Muzorewa would then be more or less under South African control, they reasoned, while seeming to be an independent black leader.

Carrington's electronic eavesdropping may also have confirmed for him the belief that Mugabe's strongest allies in the frontline states — Samora Machel in Mozambique, Kenneth Kaunda in Zambia, and Julius Nyerere in Tanzania — were exhausted from their support of the Zimbabwean guerrilla war, the interruption of trade between Zimbabwe and their countries, and the sanctions they had voluntarily applied against Smith's regime. All of them favored peace, even if it meant some compromise.

Mugabe was close to tears the evening of December 21, 1979, after finally signing the Lancaster House agreement. Certain that he could win the election, which was scheduled for the end of February, he was afraid that the British would somehow prevent him from running. And indeed, the British did not allow Mugabe to return to Zimbabwe Rhodesia until half the two-month period between the signing of the agreement and the election had elapsed.

Nkomo supporters hold their first legal rally in late 1979. In the election, the nation's blacks were to vote for 80 parliamentary seats, while the whites would vote for 20 seats. Mugabe's ZANU(PF), Nkomo's ZAPU, Sithole's ZANU, and the government's Muzorewa contended for the black seats.

A jubilant Mugabe hears the election results at his headquarters in Salisbury: Mugabe, 57 seats; Nkomo, 20; Muzorewa, 3. The landslide victory for the Marxist candidate was considered an upset, but Mugabe far outpolled his black opponents among the Shona majority. Ian Smith won all 20 white seats.

Meanwhile, an 850-man multinational peacekeeping force, headed by Britain, entered Zimbabwe Rhodesia to administer a cease-fire. They found a land devastated by war. Martial law was in effect in 95 percent of the country, and under its provisions Rhodesian troops had destroyed villages, burned crops, and reduced black civilians to near starvation. One-third of the population was living in refugee camps both inside and outside the country. There were now 70,000 troops under arms in the Rhodesian security forces and an additional 30,000 in the reserves. ZANU guerrillas inside the country numbered some 20,000, with tens of thousands more poised in camps just beyond the border in Mozambique and Botswana. Almost 8,000 people had been killed in the fighting in 1979 alone. Most white farms were deserted, the inhabitants having fled. Salisbury and most of the major cities and towns were surrounded by Zimbabwean guerrillas. With the prospect of the liberation armies' victory came the possibility that South Africa would enter the war on a massive scale. It was imperative that the cease-fire hold.

On December 28, 1979, the cease-fire went into effect. ZANU and ZAPU guerrillas began to come in from the bush to prearranged assembly points, where they would wait until the election was held. By the first week of January, 17,000 guerrillas had come in, while the government confined its forces to base. The fighting stopped; the cease-fire was a success.

Mugabe supporters celebrate the election results on the streets of Salisbury. Although the nation's blacks — and some whites — were delighted with the institution of black majority rule, many conservative whites reacted by packing their belongings and leaving the country.

Mugabe, Zimbabwe's first prime minister, embraces Canaan Banana, its first president, at Independence Day ceremonies on April 18, 1980. Britain's Lord Soames (in wig), who oversaw the cease-fire and election process, and Lord Carrington, author of the Lancaster House agreement, look on.

The next step was the election itself. There was some intimidation and violence during the campaign and later during the polling itself, with ZANU responsible for a good deal of it, but the election was relatively calm for a country that had just settled a bloody civil war. As for the candidates themselves, each felt certain of victory. Ian Smith was sure that he would win a majority of the 20 seats reserved for whites, and he planned to make certain that his choice of candidate for prime minister, Abel Muzorewa, would win the majority of the 80 black seats. The British had privately assured Smith that Mugabe would not win the election, so Smith believed that Nkomo was the only candidate who stood in Muzorewa's way. Smith began making public speeches telling Zimbabwean blacks to vote for Nkomo. As a columnist for the British newspaper the *Observer* noted, "Students of Ian Smith's political style suspect him of landing an artful blow in Joshua Nkomo's ample midriff by telling the Rhodesian masses to vote for him. As is well known, white urgings can be relied upon to evoke the opposite response from the black electorate."

Muzorewa, Smith, most whites, and many international observers believed that Muzorewa would win. He was already in place as Zimbabwe Rhodesia's prime minister, and his campaign cost more than any other election campaign ever held in Africa, with South Africa and conservative Rhodesian, British, and Americans contributing large amounts.

Rhodesia's government-controlled newspapers, radio, and television had always referred to Mugabe as the "arch-terrorist," and Smith continued to do so. Muzorewa claimed that a vote for Mugabe was a vote for a continuation of the war, and Britain, the United States, the Soviet Union, and South Africa all made it clear that they would prefer an election defeat for Mugabe, the outspoken Marxist armed by China.

On January 27, 1980, with little more than a month remaining until the election, the British allowed Mugabe to return to the country. To the astonishment of the British, the other candidates, and Mugabe himself, a crowd of 200,000 enthusiastic supporters gathered in Salisbury to greet him; a white police official said it was "the biggest crowd Rhodesia has ever seen."

In his campaign speeches, Mugabe promised to buy land from white farmers who were willing to sell and redistribute it to landless peasants. Other peasants could choose to work on government-owned cooperative farms. Women would be given equal rights under the law. He promised to raise the minimum wage so that all workers, black and white, male and female, would be paid an equal amount for equal work. Working conditions in the factories and mines would be improved, and workers would have some say in how the factories were run. All children would be guaranteed schooling, and adults who were illiterate could go to adult education classes. Government-funded health care would be made available to all citizens, regardless of their income.

> *The British government and the Rhodesian forces are hounding up our forces and making it difficult for us generally [because] they realise that we are going to win and they want to place every obstacle in our way to prevent that.*
> —ROBERT MUGABE

One of the candidates, Ndabaningi Sithole, the man who had been ousted as ZANU leader a decade before, had already registered his small party for the election under the ZANU name. Mugabe, therefore, was forced to register his party under the name ZANU(PF), for Patriotic Front, to make it clear to voters that his ZANU was the one that had fought the guerrilla war for so many years. Many whites believed — mistakenly, as it would turn out — that black voters would be confused by the similairty of the two parties' initials.

As the campaign drew to a close, Mugabe was confident. He believed that his support — drawn from the country's Shona majority, the guerrilla forces of ZANU(PF), and the thousands of refugees returning from ZANU(PF) camps in Mozambique — was strong enough to provide him with an electoral victory. He celebrated his 56th birthday, and then, the day before the election, he announced, "I'm going to win 56 seats."

Voting started on Tuesday, February 26th. It had been raining throughout the country for a month and it looked like the rain would continue through the election. Zimbabwean blacks, who knew the rain would be good for their crops, cheerfully walked through the mud to get to the polls. People started lining up at the polling stations at midnight, and by 5:00 A.M., there was a line at Salisbury's main polling station half a mile long. At 7:00 A.M., they opened. Collecting votes took a long time because many voters lived in remote rural areas, and mobile voting trucks had to cover the whole country. The last people to vote were Mugabe's and Nkomo's guerrilla soldiers in the military camps. The polls closed on Friday, the 29th of February, and counting began the next morning.

At 9:00 A.M. on March 4, 1980, the election results were in. Throughout the country, people, many too poor to own radios, gathered in groups, waiting to hear whether Abel Muzorewa, Joshua Nkomo, or Robert Mugabe would be their new leader. The results were read over the radio: Smith, all 20 white seats. Nkomo, 20. Muzorewa, 3. Mugabe, 57.

It will be true democracy. This is what we have been fighting for. Power must rest with the people for the people. They must now choose their government and they will.

—ROBERT MUGABE
upon being asked whether it would be true democracy if he won the 1980 election

The British writers David Martin and Phyllis Johnson described the scene at Mugabe's election headquarters:

> At his temporary home in Salisbury, at 3 Quorn Avenue, Mugabe and his supporters cheered as the results came through. Joyful demonstrations began immediately in the African townships and outside the ZANU(PF) headquarters at 88 Manica Road, blocking traffic. The whites listened in stunned disbelief. Mugabe, the man Smith's propaganda machine had portrayed as a Marxist monster, had achieved what none of them had believed possible. Riot police with tear gas were deployed at 88 Manica Road and wisely withdrawn. Heavily-armed troops moved into the townships and armoured vehicles patrolled the streets. But the African mood was one of jubilation and not recrimination. The bitterness lay with the whites.

Thousands of blacks, a few whites among them, crowded the streets, dancing and cheering in jubilation. Peasants all over the country celebrated. In one camp, ZANU(PF) troops led a deafening cheer. "Viva President Mugabe!" they shouted repeatedly.

The other candidates were shocked. Smith called Mugabe's victory a "tremendous bombshell." Nkomo, outraged, claimed the results had been rigged by, among others, China, Mozambique, Tanzania, Britain, and the United States. Muzorewa first condemned the vote as "totally unfree and unfair," but later accepted the election results, saying "the most important thing is that we don't have persecution of the losers."

Conservative whites were shocked by the results as well — and far more frightened by them than Muzorewa. Hundreds packed their bags, collected their children from school, and headed for South Africa. White bankers, businessmen, mining company executives, civil servants, police, and military personnel submitted their resignations, put their houses up for sale, and prepared to follow those who had already left the country.

Sally went outside to join the few dozen who had gathered in Quorn Avenue to hear the news on the radio. When Mugabe left for the Government House, she was dancing in the street.
—DAVIS SMITH
Mugabe biographer, on Sally Mugabe's reaction to Mugabe's victory in the 1980 election

Jamaican reggae musician Bob Marley sang at Independence Day festivities in Salisbury. When his fans crashed through barricades to get into the stadium where he was performing, police used tear gas and truncheons to restore order — the first instance of mass violence in independent Zimbabwe.

Many predicted a bloodbath. Mugabe, some thought, would exact vengeance against whites and the thousands of blacks who fought the war on the side of the Rhodesian government. Others, like Kenneth Kaunda of Zambia, feared that South Africa would try to stage a coup with the help of conservative whites inside Rhodesia. William F. Buckley, a conservative American newspaper columnist, predicted that whites who remained in Zimbabwe would be "butchered." Although international observers all concluded that the elections were free and fair, Buckley maintained that "Mugabe's participation in the elections should not have been tolerated" and that the United States should not have allowed Zimbabwe to vote "by majority for Communist rule."

But the transition to black majority rule was peaceful, largely because of Mugabe's astute political sense. On the day after his victory was announced, Mugabe called for unity and reconciliation, saying, "It is now the time to beat our swords into ploughshares so that we can attend to the problems of developing our economy and society."

On April 17, 1980, as he was about to assume office as independent Zimbabwe's first prime minister, Mugabe broadcast a message to the people of his nation:

> Long live our Freedom.
>
> The final countdown before the launching of the new state of Zimbabwe has now begun. Only a few hours from now Zimbabwe will become a free, independent, and sovereign state . . . The march to our national independence has been a long, arduous, and hazardous one. On this march, countless lives have been lost and many sacrifices made. Death and suffering have been the price we have been called upon to pay for the final priceless reward of freedom and national independence. May I thank all of you who have had to suffer and sacrifice for the reward we are now getting.

The next morning, the official Independence Day ceremonies got under way. Thousands of Zimbabweans, many of them ZANU(PF) soldiers, assembled in Rufaro Stadium to hear a concert featuring Bob Marley, the Jamaican reggae star whose songs of black liberation were hugely popular with nationalist activists and guerrilla fighters throughout Africa. As Marley took the stage to sing his tribute to the Zimbabwean liberation struggle, thousands outside the stadium rushed through the barriers to get inside. Security police tried to move the crowds back by firing rifle shots and tear-gas canisters into the air, and when those failed they resorted to billy clubs. The performance had to stop until the clouds of tear gas engulfing the stadium could disperse. Independence Day had been somewhat marred, but it was a relatively minor incident.

That night in Salisbury, the flag of Rhodesia and the British Union Jack were lowered for the last time. Up ran the new flag of independent Zimbabwe.

You give them one man one vote and look what they do with it.
—JOSHUA NKOMO
on Mugabe's victory

6

The Killing Ground

Upon becoming prime minister, Mugabe brought many of his former opponents into the government with him, a practice that surprised and drew praise from observers both inside and outside Zimbabwe. He consulted and maintained friendly relations with Ian Smith, still the leader of the country's white minority. He also invited ZAPU party leader Joshua Nkomo — most of whose 20 parliament seats were won in Matabeleland, home of the Ndebele — to join ZANU(PF) in a coalition government. And he appointed Peter Walls, the Rhodesian army chief he had fought against for so many years, to preside over the integration of ZANU(PF) and ZAPU forces into the new national army. In the private sector, Mugabe told the business community that despite his commitment to socialism and government ownership of business enterprises, there would be no early nationalization of industries. If the businessmen stayed in Zimbabwe, he told them, they could continue to own and operate their businesses.

We were honest in the struggle, fought gallantly for what we considered were our honest objectives, and we shall be honest in peace to achieve a society where all will have a place.
—ROBERT MUGABE

Mugabe in 1982. Upon becoming prime minister he pledged to "engender a common interest that knows no race, colour, or creed" and proceeded to impress international observers by accommodating the white minority. But his handling of tensions between the Shona and Ndebele was widely criticized.

Mugabe is carried past a statue of St. Francis Xavier at Kutama Mission, his childhood home, in July 1980. Many thought that Mugabe would consolidate political power to become a strongman ruler or take vengeance on Zimbabwe's remaining whites, but neither fear materialized.

Although in the months following independence a small but significant number of the remaining white farmers were killed by renegade guerrillas, people's greatest fear — that angry blacks would unleash a bloodbath on whites — never materialized. Some whites who left Zimbabwe at independence slowly began to trickle back in. "We should have negotiated much earlier," one white farmer told an American reporter. "We could have done without the war and been at a much better advantage today."

Nevertheless, it was not long before a crisis threatened to plunge Zimbabwe into a new civil war. The strife did not involve the nation's whites, but rather the nation's two largest African groups: the 6.5 million Shona and the 1.5 million Ndebele.

At independence, Prime Minister Mugabe invited Nkomo to take the prestigious but largely ceremonial office of the presidency. Nkomo refused, but agreed instead to become minister of home affairs, a more active post but one with less stature. To ensure the loyalty of the military, Mugabe took for himself the post of defense minister, a common practice among African heads of government. The presidency was given to Canaan Banana, a prominent churchman who would prove to be an effective mediator between Mugabe and Nkomo in the years to come.

For two years, Mugabe and Nkomo held an uneasy truce at parliament sessions in Harare (the new, African name chosen for Salisbury), even as incidents of ethnic conflict in Matabeleland escalated. Relations between ZANU(PF) and ZAPU soldiers in the newly integrated army units were tense, and there were some outbreaks of violence. Many of the attacks were clearly acts of banditry, while others were directed against whites living in the district. But some of the attacks were mounted by armed insurgents against both civilian and government targets connected with ZANU(PF) in Matabeleland. Mugabe believed that the violence constituted an attempt by Nkomo to lead a ZAPU coup to overthrow the ZANU(PF) government, a claim Nkomo repeatedly denied.

> *I feel like a china ornament sitting in a showcase.*
> —JOSHUA NKOMO
> bemoaning his lack of influence in Zimbabwean politics

Joshua Nkomo was Zimbabwe's first minister of home affairs, but in 1982 Mugabe expelled him from the government when weapons were discovered on ZAPU officials' farms. ZAPU soldiers reacted by deserting the national army, violence broke out in Matabeleland, and in March 1983 Nkomo fled the country.

On February 13, 1982, Mugabe announced that security officers had found enough military equipment on farms owned by ZAPU officials to outfit 20,000 soldiers. He reacted by accusing Nkomo of plotting a coup. Four days later, although Nkomo protested that he knew nothing about a coup, Mugabe dismissed Nkomo and three other ZAPU officials from the government. Upon hearing the news thousands of former ZAPU soldiers in the integrated Zimbabwean army deserted.

Matters were made worse by a serious drought that had hit Zimbabwe earlier that year. Matabeleland, one of the driest areas of the country even in normal weather conditions, was severely affected. With farmers unable to grow enough in their parched fields to feed their family and with livestock dying by the hundreds, many of the Ndebele deserters turned to the more convenient occupation of banditry — already a fairly popular vocation among former ZANU(PF) and ZAPU guerrillas — and proceeded to victimize both black and white farmers.

To stop the violence in Matabeleland, Mugabe sent in the army's Fifth Brigade, all of whose soldiers were Shona and trained by North Korean advisers. But instead of restoring order the brigade went on a rampage, killing hundreds of former ZAPU soldiers and more than 1,500 Ndebele civilians. Several hundred more were wounded, and torture was used against many of the 400 ZAPU party officials and supporters who were detained on charges of spying and sabotage. Most of the violence against the Ndebele occurred in and around Bulawayo, Zimbabwe's second-largest city and the capital of Matabeleland. In the Ndebele language, *bulawayo* means "killing ground."

As for Nkomo himself, police confiscated his passport in early 1983 and required him to inform them each time he planned to leave his hometown. On March 8, 1983, Nkomo slipped out of the country undetected and went into self-imposed exile, first in Botswana, then in London. Soon after Nkomo's departure, the violence in Matabeleland subsided.

Ndebele civilians fleeing to Bulawayo, capital of Matabeleland, in 1983. To curb banditry and antigovernment gangs, Mugabe sent in the army's Fifth Brigade, composed entirely of Shona soldiers. As reported by human-rights workers, the brigade massacred 1,500 Ndebele civilians and tortured scores of ZAPU officials.

Mugabe tried to mend fences with Nkomo and the Ndebele by publicly stating that he desired a reconciliation with Nkomo and that he was welcome to return. On August 16, the ZAPU leader did indeed return to Zimbabwe and called for unity, and after a debate, parliament voted to allow Nkomo to retain his seat. Meanwhile Mugabe recalled his now notorious Fifth Brigade for retraining and disciplining. A few Fifth Brigade soldiers were tried and executed for their role in the massacres, although many more killings went unpunished. Peace was restored in Matabeleland, but the scars of the conflict remained. During the next few years international human-rights groups and the Ndebele themselves charged that government forces were continuing to kill, injure, and illegally detain innocent civilians in Matabeleland.

In a 1984 interview with the Zimbabwean newspaper *Moto*, Mugabe bristled when the interviewer brought up the subject of government atrocities in Matabeleland:

> These charges are made by our opponents and in some cases it is ZAPU which will have staged that kind of opposition and criticism. . . . But in fact, no one can prove there are mass graves. Where are they? If people had died in large numbers, you wouldn't even have to look for the place. It has been said that the people of Matabeleland are being starved to death, that they are being ill-treated because they are Ndebeles, that we are trying to avenge the bitterness that obtained during the times of Lobengula.
>
> If you look at the programmes in Matabeleland South, Government has gone out of its way to try and alleviate the suffering of the people there, so it is not true to say that we have tried to wipe out the people of Matabeleland.

In 1985 the Shona-Ndebele rift was still very much in evidence. In that year's elections votes were sharply divided along ethnic lines. Mugabe gained 7 seats overall, boosting his total to 64, almost all of them in Shona districts. Nkomo lost 5 seats, dropping his total to 15, but he won every Matabeleland seat. The Ndebele who experienced the army's arbitrary violence and abuse of human rights may never fully trust Mugabe or ZANU(PF) again.

Mugabe was widely criticized in the international press for the government's actions in Matabeleland and for what some saw as his callous response to accusations of atrocities against the Ndebele. Some observers believe that Mugabe used the Matabeleland crisis as an excuse for pressuring Nkomo to consider merging ZAPU with ZANU(PF) to create a single political organization that would serve as Zimbabwe's lone political party, an aim Mugabe finally achieved in 1988.

Mugabe was long an advocate of the single-party system. According to some socialist theorists, a two-party system such as the United States's, and a multiple-party system such as those of Britain, the Western European countries, Canada, and Japan are instruments by which the wealthy ensure that they keep their wealth; in a one-party socialist state, the single party is the instrument of all the people.

Mugabe's relations with Zimbabwe's white minority were cordial in the years following independence. Despite his commitment to socialism and land reform, whites continued to own most of the large farms and businesses, and held key government positions.

Most African nations adhere to the one-party system, which theoretically unites a country against the threat of dissolving along tribal lines. But some critics say that there is little true democracy in most one-party states; in Africa, the single party is often controlled by one tribal group that uses its power to subjugate other tribal groups.

Mugabe's concept of a single-party democratic state is one in which all debates would be within the party, rather than becoming the focus for conflict between two or more parties. In 1984 Mugabe was asked by a Zimbabwean newspaper reporter why he advocated such a system:

> I don't believe the multi-party state is the best way of going about a democratic system. We must recognise that we are one society, and one country with one government. We must be nationally united . . . the best way of doing it is to have one umbrella under which all shades of opinion can be accommodated and this takes place only under a one-party state.
>
> We realise that we have various opinions in the country . . . [and] under a homogenous arrangement which recognises that we are one Zimbabwe and we must be one society and within that society we are free to express our various opinions. Whether they are radical or rightist or leftist or centre it doesn't matter. At the end of the day when we share opinions and have had our exchanges of different viewpoints we must conclude that the majority view within that umbrella is what guides us. This really is in keeping with our tradition. You never have two chiefs in a given area. There is only one chief.

The short-lived Patriotic Front coalition between ZANU(PF) and ZAPU during Chimurenga II in the 1970s was the first attempt to merge the two parties. After the 1985 elections the effort was revived, as Mugabe and Nkomo began negotiations on a more permanent merger of ZANU(PF) and ZAPU. With ZAPU the representative of the Ndebele people, Mugabe recognized the need to give Nkomo a meaningful role in the formation and operation of a single party.

Many observers were surprised that Nkomo agreed to take part in the ZANU(PF)-ZAPU merger. An Nkomo aide said a "decisive factor" in Nkomo's decision to participate in the unity talks was "the need to unite the country in the face of South Africa's destabilization. You can't have a section of the population alienated at a time like this, especially in a region bordering South Africa."

As the 1980s continued, it became increasingly clear that the biggest political factor in Zimbabwe's immediate future was the presence of South Africa on its southern border. Like Mozambique, Zambia, Botswana, and Tanzania during Chimurenga II, Zimbabwe had become a frontline state, forced to walk a fine line between supporting South Africa's black nationalists and avoiding the economic and military wrath of South Africa's apartheid government, the richest and mightiest on the continent.

Sally and Robert Mugabe at a ZANU(PF) campaign rally in 1985. In that year's elections Mugabe's party won additional seats; Nkomo's sole victories came in Ndebele districts. With a huge parliamentary majority, Mugabe began pressing Nkomo to agree to a ZANU(PF)-ZAPU merger, which would make Zimbabwe a one-party state.

7

The Behemoth to the South

In 1974, 10 years after most of Africa had gained indepedence, southern Africa was still a bastion of white-minority rule. Rhodesia was ruled by Ian Smith's UDI regime, Angola and Mozambique were ruled by colonial governments answerable to the Portuguese dictatorship, and South Africa, the largest and wealthiest of all, was firmly under the control of a white apartheid government.

But in 1975 the new democratic government of Portugal granted Angola and Mozambique their independence and in 1980 Zimbabwe finally came under black rule. Despite having sent paramilitary troops to fight alongside the Rhodesian and Portuguese colonial armies in the Zimbabwean, Angolan, and Mozambican liberation struggles, the South Africans had failed to stop the installation of black rule in those countries. South Africa, already ostracized by most of the nations of the world, was left utterly alone.

> *When we became independent, we realised that we had inherited a situation which tied us to South Africa, economically and politically— militarily as well.*
> —ROBERT MUGABE
> 1982

Mozambican refugee children in 1987. Military attacks and economic disruptions engineered by the white apartheid regime of South Africa against its black-ruled neighbors caused great hardship in Zimbabwe and the rest of the region throughout the 1980s.

Members of the African National Congress (ANC), the organization dedicated to ending apartheid in South Africa, at a Harare rally on behalf of Nelson Mandela, the ANC leader imprisoned by the white regime for 25 years. Mugabe's support for the ANC resulted in the bombing of Zimbabwe by the South African military.

South Africa's ultraconservative white regime had long feared the isolation in which it found itself at the dawn of the 1980s. The apartheid government had always operated on the principle that it was under siege from the country's black, Asian, and mixed-race majority — which by 1980 outnumbered the whites by 26 million to 6 million. Now South Africa was threatened from outside as well, surrounded by liberated black nations and cut off from the rest of the world culturally, politically, and to some extent, economically.

At various times throughout the 1980s, the South African military bombed or raided all of the countries on its borders, and some well beyond. As a result of the attacks, civilians were killed in Angola, Botswana, Lesotho, Mozambique, Swaziland, Zambia, and Zimbabwe. In May 1986 and again in May 1987, South Africa bombed Harare, killing scores of Zimbabweans and causing millions of dollars of damage. South Africa justified the bombings by claiming that Zimbabwe and its neighbors represent a threat to South Africa. Botswana's foreign minister Gaositwe Chiepe ridiculed this claim, made after Botswana's capital was bombed in 1985, when she pointed out that there are more people in South Africa's 1 million–man army than in the entire population of Botswana.

Besides overt military attacks, South Africa has tried more subtle methods of destabilizing neighboring black governments. As the British writer Joseph Hanlon points out, Zimbabwe in the early days of independence was a frequent South African target. On December 18, 1981, a bomb exploded at ZANU(PF) national headquarters in Harare, killing 7 and injuring 124. The bomb was timed to go off during a meeting of the party's central committee, but because the meeting had been delayed Mugabe and his top ministers escaped unharmed. Immediately after the bombing, Mugabe's head of security — a white named Geoffrey Price, who had been a leading figure in Ian Smith's security forces — fled to South Africa. Four months earlier there had been an incident almost as dramatic, after a Zimbabwean army ammunition dump outside Harare was blown up. A white army officer who had served in the Rhodesian forces during the war was arrested on charges of sabotage, but a South African commando team kidnapped the wife and children of the Zimbabwean official investigating the case and held them hostage. The Zimbabweans had to exchange the white officer for the investigator's family.

The reasons behind South Africa's attacks on neighboring countries are complex. When a Zimbabwean asked black South African archbishop and 1984 Nobel Peace Prize–winner Desmond Tutu how South Africa's neighbors could help black South Africans win majority rule, Tutu answered, "Be a success." The South African government justified white-minority rule by claiming that black Africans are incapable of governing themselves, that they would massacre whites if they were allowed to take over, and that they would destroy the economy. But there were examples, such as Zimbabwe, that refuted that claim, and the South African position was weakened.

Nevertheless, South Africa continued to subvert the black governments of its neighbors throughout the 1980s. In addition to announced, as well as secret, military attacks, South Africa applied economic pressure. Most of southern Africa's import and export routes pass through South Africa — a legacy of the colonial period, when the British built railroads and highways to transport minerals and

Mugabe with Zambian leader Kenneth Kaunda in 1980. In the 1980s Zimbabwe joined the frontline states — Zambia, Tanzania, Mozambique, Botswana, and Angola — in harboring anti-apartheid forces. But dependence on South African trade and fear of military reprisal forced them to limit their efforts.

other goods to South African ports. Thus all the countries in southern Africa are dependent on South Africa economically — and none more so than Zimbabwe.

When black majority rule became a reality in Zimbabwe in 1980, 94 percent of the nation's imports and exports went through South Africa, and in the late 1980s that figure still stood as high as 85 percent. If Zimbabwe decided to give South Africa's main opposition group, the African National Congress, the kind of aid that Mozambique gave ZANU(PF) during Chimurenga II, South Africa could easily cripple the Zimbabwean economy.

In 1980, in an attempt to lessen their economic dependence on the South African regime they oppose, the black-ruled nations of southern Africa organized the Southern African Development Coordination Conference (SADCC). Zimbabwe, as the least impoverished nation in the group — the other members were Angola, Botswana, Lesotho, Malawi, Mozambique, Swaziland, Tanzania, and Zambia, all impoverished countries — was given responsibility for promoting agricultural development.

SADCC's plans hinged on being able to import and export through Mozambique and Angola, which have good deep-water ports and which are hundreds of miles closer to most SADCC countries than South Africa, and therefore much cheaper. Not surprisingly, South Africa concentrated its attacks on SADCC's two routes to the sea to prevent its black-ruled neighbors from becoming economically independent. For example, South Africa invaded Angola several times in the 1980s, once with more than 20,000 troops, and paid 90 percent of the funds for a guerrilla movement, the National Union for Total Independence of Angola (UNITA), which caused more than $10 billion worth of damage to Angolan roads and rail lines.

South Africa also raided Mozambique several times, and it used a right-wing guerrilla organization, the Mozambique National Resistance (RENAMO), to damage that country's roads and rail lines to the sea. RENAMO was created in 1974 by the Portuguese secret police and the Rhodesian Central

White Rhodesian soldiers near the end of the Second Chimurenga in 1980. Some joined the South African–supported RENAMO guerrillas, committed to disrupting black-ruled Marxist Mozambique. By 1987, RENAMO and South African attacks had made Mozambique the world's poorest nation.

Intelligence Organization in a last-ditch effort to stop FRELIMO and its leader, Samora Machel, from winning the Mozambican liberation war.

In the late 1970s, with Chimurenga II still raging, RENAMO was based in Rhodesia. But when Robert Mugabe came to power in 1980, he gave RENAMO 72 hours to leave the country, which they did, only to resurface in South Africa. The South African department of military intelligence gave them weapons and vehicles and encouraged them to begin a bombing campaign to cripple Mozambique's ports, railways, villages, medical centers, schools, churches, and development projects.

In 1982, Mugabe sent Zimbabwean troops into Mozambique to assist that country in defending itself against RENAMO attacks. By 1987 there were 12,000 Zimbabwean soldiers in Mozambique, representing 30 percent of the Zimbabwean military and approximately 10 percent of the national budget. RENAMO responded by making raids into Zimbabwe, killing 100 villagers who lived near the Mozambican border in 1987 alone.

Within Mozambique itself, RENAMO had devastated the already impoverished country. According to a 1988 report by the U.S. State Department, the South African–backed organization had massacred some 100,000 Mozambican civilians in the previous 2 years, causing an additional 2 million Mozambicans to flee to refugee camps both inside and outside the country's borders. Since 1981, RENAMO had destroyed one-third of Mozambique's health clinics and one-third of its schools. RENAMO attacks had forced the abandonment of farms throughout the countryside, causing widespread fa-

Mugabe in Washington, D.C., with U.S. president Ronald Reagan in 1983. During the 1980s Mugabe was often critical of U.S. policy toward the Third World and South Africa; Reagan and the U.S. government responded by sharply cutting back U.S. aid to Zimbabwe.

Mugabe with outgoing U.S. president Jimmy Carter in Washington, D.C., in 1980. Carter, of all U.S. presidents perhaps the most responsive to African concerns, pledged millions of dollars of aid to restore Zimbabwe's war-ravaged economy.

mine, and the annual income of the average Mozambican had been cut in half, down to $95 per year — the lowest such figure of any country in the world. As ominous for Mugabe were allegations that RENAMO operations were still being run by former Rhodesian army officers who could conceivably bring the same type of mass terror to Zimbabwe.

In addition to aiding Mozambique, Mugabe and the Zimbabwean government took the forefront in urging Britain, the United States, and the rest of the international community to refrain from trading with South Africa altogether. British and U.S. corporations supplied South Africa with oil, automobiles, and computer technology, and neither the British nor the U.S. government took even a moderately strong stance against the South African regime until the late 1980s.

In a ceremony held on July 4, 1986, at the U.S. embassy in Harare, a high Zimbabwean official strongly criticized the United States for refusing to impose sanctions on South Africa. Former U.S. president Jimmy Carter, whose administration was generally conceded to have been more sympathetic to African concerns than any other in U.S. history, walked out on the speech, calling it "an insult to my country and to me personally." Carter left before he had a chance to hear another Zimbabwean official, who commented that it was strange that "as the American people celebrate freedom from colonial rule and unrepresentative government . . . millions of the wretched, poor, and oppressed in South Africa will be answering for their desire for freedom with their very lives."

Mugabe agreed with President Carter that the opening speech was "inappropriate" and apologized to Carter. He refused, however, to apologize to U.S. president Ronald Reagan for criticizing Reagan's refusal to impose sanctions. Reagan retaliated by drastically cutting U.S. aid to Zimbabwe.

In the early 1980s, when both Mugabe and Reagan were new to their job as leader of their country, the relationship between Zimbabwe and the United States had been cordial. One of Mugabe's first acts as prime minister was to organize a large fund-raising event in which the nations of the world were asked to contribute money toward rebuilding war-drained Zimbabwe. The United States agreed to pledge $225 million during a 3-year period. To the delight of the strongly anti-Soviet Reagan, Mugabe did not invite the Soviet Union to participate — mainly because the Soviets had backed Nkomo during the liberation war.

Zimbabwe was regarded as a shining example by the poor nations of the world, and Mugabe agreed. At the United Nations, Zimbabwean delegates took the lead as spokespeople for the Third World, often objecting to American policies. Reagan and the U.S. government officials believed that such action showed ingratitude in light of the U.S. aid Zim-

South African police at the wreck of a Mozambican jetliner that crashed in October 1986, killing Mozambican president Machel and 27 others. Evidence suggested that the South African government shot down the plane to assassinate Machel.

babwe had received. In the 3 years that culminated with the July 4, 1986, incident, the Reagan administration reduced U.S. aid to Zimbabwe from $90 million a year to virtually nothing. Still, Mugabe continued to be an outspoken critic of U.S. foreign policy, particularly in South Africa.

In October 1986, an event occurred that presented Mugabe with a great personal tragedy and also underscored the South African government's determination to do whatever was necessary to weaken the countries surrounding it.

On the evening of October 20, a Mozambican airliner carrying Samora Machel, many of his top advisers, and several Mozambican intellectuals, crashed inside South Africa under mysterious circumstances. South African minister of defense Magnus Malan, just days before the crash, had made statements that many interpreted as a threat against Machel's life. Furthermore, a small encampment of South African soldiers was set up at the site of the crash, out in the wilderness — a few days before the crash occurred. They were in position to take the plane's flight recorder and all of the documents on board. More than five hours passed before the injured survivors were taken to the hospital and Mozambique was notified about the crash. Several of the survivors later said they heard a loud noise like an explosion just before the plane went down.

Initial South African reports about the crash were misleading. Government spokesmen claimed the plane had gone down in a storm, though weather records and local witnesses confirmed that the skies were clear that evening. An autopsy report stated that one victim's throat had been slit as a result of the crash, but a survivor later said that he had lain next to the victim for several hours before they were rescued, and that the man was alive with his throat intact when they were both taken to a South African hospital. Some survivors reported that South African emergency workers had promised to take them to a hospital reserved for whites instead of the poorly equipped and overcrowded hospital for blacks — if they would agree to join RENAMO.

Although no evidence ever surfaced proving conclusively that South Africa caused the crash to occur, the people of Zimbabwe were convinced that South Africa was responsible for the assassination of Machel. When the news of his death was announced, thousands of Zimbabweans in Harare rioted in the worst violence in Harare since independence. Hundreds of students, many carrying signs proclaiming Samora Machel, We Will Avenge You, ran through the streets and attacked South Africa's trade mission and airline offices. The rioters also stoned the U.S. embassy in response to what they saw as that country's support for South Africa.

Despite the steady deterioration of the racial situation inside South Africa and the increasing isolation of the apartheid regime, Zimbabwe was in a precarious position. The threat that the increasingly desperate South African government would step up military attacks and economic pressure against Zimbabwe and the other black-ruled nations of southern Africa presented Mugabe with his most stubborn and dangerous problem as the 1980s drew to a close.

Zimbabweans protest the death of Samora Machel by calling for the death of South African president P. W. Botha. Some protesters stoned the U.S. embassy in Harare to express their displeasure with what they felt was the U.S. government's failure to act against South Africa's white apartheid regime.

8

"We Leave Behind Us a United Country"

Most international observers were impressed with Zimbabwe's economic record in the first eight years of Mugabe's rule. Despite having suffered the hardships of a long and bloody civil war, the flight of many of the nation's wealthiest and most experienced people after the installation of black-majority rule and constant harassment by South Africa, Zimbabwe's economy remained one of the healthiest in black Africa. Mugabe successfully instituted a health-care program that cut the infant-mortality rate in half and an education campaign that saw the construction of hundreds of schools and a rise in primary-school enrollment from 40 percent to 93 percent. He doubled the minimum wage, lowered the price of food to make it affordable to the poor, and instituted a number of other initiatives that have dramatically improved the quality of life for many Zimbabweans. The nation remained one of the world's most efficient producers of corn, sugarcane, cattle, and tobacco, and continued to earn considerable revenue through the mining of gold and coal.

Zimbabwe cannot just be a country of blacks. It is and should remain our country, all of us together.
—ROBERT MUGABE

Sally and Robert Mugabe at the opening of Parliament. In 1988 Mugabe finally realized his dream of a one-party system when he persuaded Nkomo to allow ZAPU to be absorbed into ZANU(PF). The merger left Mugabe in control of 99 out of 100 parliamentary seats.

Mugabe addressing the United Nations in New York in 1987. Recognized as one of the Third World's most capable leaders, Mugabe served a 3-year term as chairman of the Nonaligned Movement, the organization of approximately 100 nations allied to neither Washington nor Moscow.

But for all the successes, it is nowhere near what Mugabe originally hoped to accomplish. From the start, his vision for Zimbabwe was one of a socialist society in which all people had equal access to land, women had equal rights and opportunities, children were given free education, and everyone had equal access to health care, unemployment benefits, and old-age pensions. Mugabe also envisioned peasants working together on cooperative farms and sharing the cost of machinery, tools, fertilizer, and seeds so that all could farm more efficiently. Similarly, factory workers might own the factories they worked in or participate in decisions concerning the factories and profits.

But Mugabe has chosen to lead Zimbabwe very gradually toward these goals. The result has been that Zimbabwe's economy is still relatively healthy, but there is considerable poverty, inequality, and landlessness. After independence, some foreign-owned corporations remained in Zimbabwe, occupying large tracts of land. White farms, some of them as large as 3,000 acres, continued to operate. And as the American writer David Lamb points out, the Zimbabwean government "has paid fair-market prices to whites who sold their farms and left the country, unable to tolerate a place where black cabinet ministers called each other 'comrade'." The government's policy has been to take the land it buys and redistribute it among peasant farmers.

But Mugabe faced a number of problems in redistributing land. Available land of good quality was scarce, and whites who were willing to sell charged high prices. By 1988, 40 percent of Zimbabwe's farmland was still owned by a few white farmers.

Some peasants have done quite well in independent Zimbabwe, while others with fewer resources have not. A few peasants had enough money at independence to buy farms from white settlers, and they are prospering. Many peasants have voluntarily joined agricultural programs sponsored by the government, including collective farms where farmers work together, share tractors or plows, and divide the costs and profits among themselves. Others, particularly former guerrilla soldiers, pooled their demobilization pay and formed cooperative farms without government assistance. At the bottom of the scale are people who have no land. Many simply moved onto white-owned farmland without permission and began farming. Until 1987 the Mugabe government did not evict these squatters.

More than 70 percent of the farmers in Zimbabwe, as in most of Africa, are women. Most women farm without sophisticated machinery: Often all they have is a hoe. Farming in itself is a full-time job, but women must also walk long distances, often miles, to get fresh water and firewood, and must spend many more hours washing clothes and preparing food over open fires; few houses in Zimbabwe have electricity or running water. At the same time women must care for their children.

Deliberately we were slow in the policy of socialisation because we felt we had first to create as formidable a base for the launching for our socialist programmes and even then, in launching them, we also must be calculating sufficiently so that we didn't, as it were, in the process overthrow the infrastructure, destroy it in order to carry out the programmes which are ideologically oriented.
—ROBERT MUGABE

> *It is our view that women have been doubly oppressed in this country. Firstly they suffered the general oppression which the men have suffered and, secondly, the men are responsible for oppressing the women.*
>
> —ROBERT MUGABE

But unlike most Third World countries, Zimbabwe has undertaken an aggressive program to guarantee equal rights for women. The nation has a one-person, one-vote system, so all adult women can vote. In 1981, discriminatory wage scales were eliminated so that women could be paid on the same scale as their male counterparts. Women are now given 3 months of guaranteed maternity leave, during which they continue to receive health benefits, and a few qualify to receive 75 percent of their regular salary during their pregnancy. In 1982, the Legal Age of Majority Act was passed, giving all women more than 18 years old the same adult status as men; during the colonial era, all women, no matter what their age, education, or income, were treated as legal minors without the right to take out loans, sign contracts, have legal custody of their own children, or choose how the money they earned was to be spent. Another new law made it mandatory that property be divided equally between men and women in a divorce. At independence, 2 cabinet ministers out of 26, 2 deputy ministers out of 11, and 9 of the 80 black members of parliament were women. With Sally Mugabe often at the head of various commissions, the Zimbabwean government has repeatedly demonstrated its willingness to give women's rights a high priority.

An incident in 1986 demonstrated her husband's commitment to women's equality. The president of Iran, Mohammed Ali Khamenei, toured Africa in late 1985 and early 1986, offering to sell oil to petroleum-starved African countries at less than the world-market price. One of Khamenei's preconditions, however, was that women had to cover their head at gatherings he attended; furthermore they were not to be included in receiving lines and were to be seated alone at the back of the gathering. Several African countries complied with Khameini's demand.

But when Khameini visited Zimbabwe, Mugabe refused, seating two Zimbabwean women dignitaries at the head table. The Iranian delegation did not come to the banquet, prompting Zimbabwean foreign minister Witness Mangwende to tell the gathering:

The major role played by Zimbabwean women during the war of liberation and the role they continue to play in the overall development of our country, entitle them to an equal status and standing in every respect with their male counterparts — a principle on which the government of Zimbabwe is unable and indeed unwilling to compromise.

Mugabe's dealings with the economy, with women's rights, with relations between the Shona and the Ndebele, and with South Africa and international affairs are vital to Zimbabwe's future. In addition, he faces a potential crisis in the rapidly rising population, which will have grown from 8 million in 1980 to 10 million in 1990. He must also contend with the alarming spread of AIDS, the disease that has ravaged black Africa throughout the 1980s; the first AIDS cases in Zimbabwe were reported in 1983 and could affect thousands by the mid-1990s. But despite the importance of all these issues, there is one subject that preoccupies the Western press: the black majority government's relationship with Zimbabwe's white minority.

Sally Mugabe speaking in Nairobi, Kenya, at a 1985 UN conference on the status of women. She and her husband have led their nation's efforts to give full civil rights to women. By the end of the 1980s, Zimbabwe was recognized as one of the world's most advanced nations in women's rights.

As the American journalist Sanford J. Ungar points out, the number of white farmers increased, much to everyone's surprise, in the period immediately following Mugabe's ascension to the prime ministership. Rhodesian government and military officials, whose policies against the black population were often brutal and led to the death of thousands, were allowed to stay in the country and even to receive their pensions. As Ungar writes:

> The wealthiest white families still lived in great comfort, even splendor, with plenty of black servants. Indeed, one fact that tells a great deal about how limited was the initial transformation of Zimbabwe's economy is that three years after independence "domestic service" was still its third largest employment category.
>
> Nothing could be a more poignant symbol than the grand home of Ian Smith in the still mostly white suburbs of Harare. There, in the midst of a finely sculpted garden and in a house filled with bric-a-brac and mementos of his controversial career, he graciously received visitors and held forth with impunity on the sins of the Mugabe government.

Ndabaningi Sithole in 1978. In 1986 he left Zimbabwe for South Africa, where he broadcast anti-Mugabe messages; later the former ZANU leader was denied asylum in the United States. Former Rhodesian prime minister Ian Smith, after a run-in with the Zimbabwean authorities, retired from politics but continued to live in Harare.

Despite the fact that Mugabe remained true to his word about preserving the rights of the white minority, by 1985 there were only 100,000 left in Zimbabwe. The whites who remained chose to play less and less of a role in the nation's politics. Only 34,000 whites voted in the 1985 election, and Smith's ultraconservative party lost 5 of the 20 seats he had controlled in the 1980 election. By 1987 there was only one white in Mugabe's cabinet.

In 1982 Smith and Mugabe clashed, but Mugabe seems to have deliberately handled the situation in a way that would not antagonize the white community. After Smith made a speech in the United States asking Americans not to give aid to the Mugabe government and claiming that standards for education and health had declined under the black majority government, Mugabe ordered the confiscation of his Zimbabwean passport. Smith's house was searched and his collection of guns removed, prompting Smith to state that he was a victim of persecution. Most observers scoffed, but when Bishop Abel Muzorewa was briefly detained in 1983 on charges of subversion, many wondered whether Mugabe was conducting a crackdown on his political opponents. But in both Smith's and Muzorewa's case Mugabe backed off after an initial show of force.

In 1987, after Smith urged white South Africans to stand behind that country's government in opposing international sanctions, the Zimbabwean parliament voted 38 to 10 to suspend him from his seat for a year. That suspension seemed to mark the end of Smith's political career, and in many ways the end of significant white participation in the Zimbabwean government.

According to the terms of the Lancaster House agreement, 1987 was also the year the 20 parliament seats reserved for whites would be abolished. On August 21, 1987, the parliament voted 78 to 0 to abolish reserved white seats. Eight of those voting to abolish white seats were themselves white. Twelve whites abstained because of a procedural question, although they had agreed in principle to the turnover of the white seats.

> *The West doesn't like opposition, they do not want people who are strong-willed and who have got opinions of their own. We cannot be puppets. We refused to be puppets in fighting the war and getting rid of injustice. We did not do so in order to invite the West or the East to be masters on us.*
> —ROBERT MUGABE

The frontline leaders in 1982 (left to right): Sam Nujoma of the Namibian guerrillas, Kaunda of Zambia, Machel of Mozambique, Julius Nyerere of Tanzania, Mugabe, and dos Santos of Angola. In the 1980s, South African efforts to disrupt Zimbabwean life included sabotage and the arming of Ndebele rebels in Matabeleland.

The black and white members of parliament present for the vote, dressed in their formal parliamentary black robes and white wigs, sang and danced in the aisles to celebrate. Justice Minister Eddison Zvobgo announced, "This is not a vote against whites. On the contrary this action will show that all Zimbabweans can vote together. We will forget race from now on and get on with our national development."

Another incident in 1987 marked a turning point for Zimbabwean whites — and in the continuing bitterness between the Shona and the Ndebele. In Matabeleland in November of that year 16 whites on a missionary-run farm were killed by an ax-wielding gang claiming to be "Marxist-Leninist guerrillas" opposed to the Mugabe government. The massacre brought to 24 the number of white farmers killed in racial incidents in Matabeleland during the previous 6 months; by contrast, only 12 white farmers in the province were killed from 1973 through 1980, the height of the war.

The killers were apparently reacting to the newly instituted government policy of evicting squatters from white-owned farmland. Some 40,000 squatters, mostly in Matabeleland, had been removed during 1987, prompting a renewal of anti-Shona sentiment among the Ndebele. Earlier that year, Richard Gwesala, the leader of a group of Ndebele outlaws thought to be responsible for 70 murders in Matabeleland, was killed by government forces. According to press reports, his body was put on display in the town of Gweru to dispel widespread belief among the Ndebele that he had supernatural powers; thousands came to view the body. The situation was complicated by South Africa's practice of supplying arms to Ndebele outlaws.

President Banana and his wife Janet with Robert and Sally Mugabe. Although Banana's post as president was purely ceremonial, he proved a skilled mediator between Mugabe and Nkomo during the three years of fractious negotiations that led up to the ZANU(PF)-ZAPU merger.

At the time of the missionary massacre, Mugabe and Nkomo were once again negotiating a ZANU–ZAPU merger. The talks had been going on without success for almost three years, because, according to most reports, Mugabe was unwilling to make any major compromises. As in 1982, Nkomo had to endure accusations that he was somehow behind the killings. He called them "an atrocious, evil, vicious act," adding that "each time we get close to unity something like this happens. We have enemies who want to see Zimbabwe torn to pieces, be they agents of South Africa or of groups within the country."

The pressure was already on Nkomo to accept Mugabe's plan for a ZANU–ZAPU merger; in September of 1987 most ZAPU political activities were forbidden and the party's headquarters were shut down. The Matabeleland killings seemed to prompt Nkomo to accept Mugabe's terms. With President Banana acting as mediator, as he had throughout the three years of talks, Mugabe and Nkomo announced a joint agreement for the merger on December 22, 1987. ZANU and ZAPU would join together as a single party, ZANU, led by Mugabe, with Nkomo serving in a vice-presidential post. All members of the party would pledge their support for the creation of a one-party state committed to the establishment of "a socialist society" in Zimbabwe.

Nkomo seemed to have agreed to the merger in the hope it would reduce ethnic tensions by bringing the Shona and Ndebele together in one political organization. "We do not want to leave behind a legacy of division," he said at the signing ceremony. "We want to lay the foundation of a Zimbabwe with one people, one nation."

For Mugabe, it was both a political and a personal victory, clearing the way for the establishment of the socialist state he had always sought. "This occasion fills me with emotion," he said at the ceremony. "We can now move into the future hand in hand, knowing that we leave behind us a united country, instead of going to our graves separately leaving behind us a divided country."

On January 2, 1988, the actual transformation of the government took place. The post of prime minister was abolished and the presidency was made the top office in the nation. Accordingly, Mugabe became president of Zimbabwe; he also stepped down from the defense ministry and gave it to a longtime Ndebele political ally. Nkomo, meanwhile, was named minister of rural and urban development and one of the nation's two vice-presidents.

It marked the end of Zimbabwe's infancy. Over the course of his long struggle to lead his nation, Robert Mugabe had been tough when he had to be and conciliatory when he had to be. He had endured much criticism, both at home and abroad, but much praise as well. Recognized as one of the Third World's most eloquent and effective leaders, Mugabe prepared to guide Zimbabwe into the 1990s.

After 25 years of rivalry, Mugabe and Nkomo agreed to unite their followers at the beginning of 1988. The government was restructured, with Mugabe becoming a U.S.-style president and Nkomo one of two vice-presidents. The two men pledged their commitment to building a socialist, democratic Zimbabwe under a one-party system.

Further Reading

Astrow, Andre. *Zimbabwe: A Revolution That Lost Its Way?* London: Zed, 1983.

Austin, Reg. *Racism and Apartheid in Southern Africa: Rhodesia.* Paris: UNESCO Press, 1975.

Beach, D. N. *The Shona and Zimbabwe: 900–1850.* New York: Holmes & Meier, 1980.

Hudson, Miles. *Triumph or Tragedy? Rhodesia to Zimbabwe.* London: Hamish Hamilton, 1982.

Kapunga, Leonard. *Rhodesia: The Struggle for Freedom.* New York: Orbis, 1974.

Keppel-Jones, Arthur. *Rhodes & Rhodesia.* Kingston, Ont.: McGill-Queens University Press, 1983.

Lessing, Doris. *African Stories.* New York: Ballantine, 1965. [Fiction]

Martin, D., and P. Johnson. *Destructive Engagement: Southern Africa at War.* Harare: Zimbabwe Publishing House, 1986.

Mason, Philip. *The Birth of a Dilemma.* New York: Oxford University Press, 1958.

Miambo, Eshmael Ephial Mtshumayeli. *The Struggle for a Birthright.* London: Hurst, 1972.

Moore, Robin. *Rhodesia.* New York: Condor, 1977.

Mugabe, Robert Gabriel. *Our Way of Liberation.* Gweru, Zimbabwe: Mambo Press, 1983.

O'Callaghan, Marion. *Southern Rhodesia: The Effects of a Conquest Society on Education, Culture and Information.* Paris: UNESCO Press, 1977.

O'Meara, Patrick. *Rhodesia.* Ithaca: Cornell University Press, 1975.

Ranger, T. O. *The African Voice in Southern Rhodesia: 1898–1930.* Evanston, IL: Northwestern University Press, 1970.

Reed, Douglas. *The Battle for Rhodesia.* Greenwich, CT: Devin-Adair, 1967.

Shamuyarira, Nathan M. *Crisis in Rhodesia.* Albuquerque, NM: Transatlantic Arts, 1966.

Smith, David et al. *Mugabe.* Harare, Zimbabwe: Pioneer Head, 1981.

Thompson, Carol B. *Challenge to Imperialism: The Frontline States and the Liberation of Zimbabwe.* London: Westview Press, 1985.

Wills, A. J. *An Introduction to the History of Central Africa.* London: Oxford University Press, 1973.

Chronology

Feb. 12, 1924	Born Robert Gabriel Mugabe in Kutama Mission, Rhodesia
1949	Begins studies at Fort Hare University, South Africa
1957	Goes to newly independent Ghana to teach
1960	Returns to Rhodesia with Sally Heyfron, whom he later marries
July 20, 1960	Joins National Democratic Party (NDP)
Oct. 1960	Elected NDP publicity secretary
Jan. 7, 1961	Joshua Nkomo elected NDP leader
Dec. 9, 1961	Rhodesian government bans the NDP
Dec. 17, 1961	Nkomo and NDP leadership form Zimbabwe African People's Union (ZAPU)
Sept. 19, 1962	Prime Minister Whitehead bans ZAPU; police arrest Mugabe
Dec. 1962	Winston Field elected prime minister
1963	Nkomo suspends four members of the ZAPU leadership including Mugabe; the suspended leaders form Zimbabwe African National Union (ZANU)
1964	Field resigns; Ian Smith becomes prime minister, bans ZANU, orders arrest of Mugabe and other ZANU leaders; ZANU begins guerrilla operations against the Smith government
Nov. 11, 1965	Smith announces Rhodesia's Unilateral Declaration of Independence
1966	Mugabe, still in detention, is transferred to Salisbury prison; ZANU escalates guerrilla war
1968	UN bans trade with Rhodesia
1974	Mugabe, released from detention, leaves for Mozambique to establish a ZANU base
1975	Nkomo and ZAPU join ZANU forces in Mozambique; ZANU and ZAPU form Zimbabwe People's Army
1976	Zimbabwe People's Army splits into ZAPU and ZANU
1978	Smith proposes Internal Settlement; Mugabe and Nkomo reject plan; Bishop Abel Muzorewa, a black nationalist leader, accepts settlement
May 1979	Muzorewa becomes prime minister in accord with the Internal Settlement
Sept.–Dec. 1979	Mugabe negotiates and signs the Lancaster House agreement
March 4, 1980	Mugabe elected prime minister
April 17, 1980	Zimbabwe achieves independence
Feb. 17, 1982	Mugabe-Nkomo rift; massacres in Matabeleland
May 1986	South Africa bombs Harare
Jan. 2, 1988	Zimbabwe officially becomes a one-party state

Index

Lorraine Eide received a B.A. in political science from Middlebury College, Vermont. She has studied African history and politics at Oxford University and the Institute of African Studies, Columbia University, from which she received an M.Phil. in comparative politics in 1987 and where she continues to study toward her doctorate.

Arthur M. Schlesinger, jr., taught history at Harvard for many years and is currently Albert Schweitzer Professor of the Humanities at City University of New York. He is the author of numerous highly praised works in American history and has twice been awarded the Pulitzer Prize. He served in the White House as special assistant to Presidents Kennedy and Johnson.

PICTURE CREDITS